What
You
Should
Know
About
Church
History

What
You
Should
Know
About
Church
History

CHARLENE
ALTEMOSE,
MSC

Liguori

ONE LIGUORI DRIVE
LIGUORI MO 63057-9999

Imprimi Potest:
Richard Thibodeau, C.Ss.R.
Provincial, Denver Province
The Redemptorists

Imprimatur:
Most Reverend Timothy M. Dolan
Auxiliary Bishop, Archdiocese of St. Louis

ISBN 0-7648-0818-4
Library of Congress Catalog Card Number: 2001098386

© 2002, Charlene Altemose, MSC
Printed in the United States of America
02 03 04 05 06 5 4 3 2 1

All rights reserved. No part of this book may be reproduced, stored
in a retrieval system, or transmitted without the written permission
of Liguori Publications.

Scripture quotations are from the *New Revised Standard Version of
the Bible,* © 1989 by the Division of Christian Education of the
National Council of the Churches of Christ in the USA. Used with
permission. All rights reserved.

To order, call 1-800-325-9521
www.liguori.org
www.catholicbooksonline.com

Contents

Introduction

The Pilgrim Church

Our Church is a pilgrim Church, and one way to think of our Church story is to experience it as a pilgrimage. On our trip back in time we'll visit sacred times, places, events, and people. We'll watch the Roman Catholic Church grow from an insignificant Jewish sect to the universal faith influence it is today.

Rather than reviewing dry historical details, see this pilgrimage as a journey that happens now. See the hand of God in each person, place, and event. In this way, we come to understand how the past shapes our present life as Catholics.

We come to this pilgrimage as individuals, with our own personal experiences of the Church. We belong to a body of believers who share a common faith, but each Catholic has a unique perception of that faith. Join your experience with the enthusiasm, heroism, hardships, and difficulties of times past. You begin on your terms, but you blend your faith with the collective wisdom and faith life of those who have pursued the same quest through the centuries since the birth of Christ. May you complete this pilgrimage renewed in mind and spirit, grateful for our Catholic heritage.

Your pilgrimage is a twofold journey: you journey not only into time past but also into the depths of your own soul. Pilgrimage challenges you to growth, conversion, and a deeper relationship with God. Relive this journey, and like a pilgrim, be renewed and refreshed.

Preparing for
Pilgrimage

Just as traditional pilgrims wear distinctive garments, clothe yourself, too, in distinctive pilgrim attire—the mantle of faith. Believe wholeheartedly that the Church as God's revelation is the continuing presence of Jesus who promised, "I am with you always." Pilgrimage will only profit you if you have faith. Believe that the Church is God's plan for you, the way you come to God.

Put on the sandals of empathy. Walk in the footsteps of those who have gone before. Try to understand the world of a particular time, so different from your own. See the Church at work in different times, in different ways than you experience. Relive the Catholic faith life of people of other lands and other times.

Don the broad-brimmed pilgrim hat of open-mindedness. Accept the unique character of each age. Notice how the Church adapts the Christian message to the circumstances and the needs of each age. Be broad in your thinking as you encounter faith practices of the past.

Just as pilgrims display their distinct insignia—a scallop shell, the baptismal symbol of rebirth and resurrection—you, too, carry the emblem of your allegiance to the Church, your baptismal commitment. May your faith be renewed on this pilgrimage.

Travel light, and embark on the journey unencumbered by anything that hinders your total involvement. Get rid of superfluous baggage—petty prejudices and stereotypes of the Church. Be clearsighted, ready to experience the Church of each age with eyes of gratitude and wonder.

Carry with you the pilgrim staff of prayer. Ask the Holy Spirit to steady your faith as you encounter unfamiliar Church stories and practices. Pray that you will be open and aware of new insights through the gifts of understanding and wisdom.

Realize that, as with any pilgrimage, you are leaving the comfort zone of your own ideas about the Church. Discover the Church as it appears within various cultures in its human dimension, often far from ideal. The Church too is a pilgrim, on the way toward fulfillment in the reign of God. Be ready for the challenge of confronting sinful practices, scandals, bad judgments, and evils that are part of our faith story. Be prepared for pleasant surprises as you experience heroism and fervent faith along the way. You may make a new discovery about the Church and about your own faith, aware of the divine guidance of the Holy Spirit.

Like pilgrims who seek respite in hostels along the way, we pause after each five hundred years of Church history and sift through the souvenirs and memories of that specific era. Ask yourself what you can learn from that epoch and how the events of that past time enrich your faith today. Reflect on the inspiration and gallant efforts of the many heroes and saints who are part of the Catholic Church story. Think of the hardships, sacrifices, and challenges the Church experiences in that time. See how time and again, when the Church seems at its lowest, it overcomes hardships and continues the mission of Christ steadfastly and with determination.

As pilgrims receive a special blessing before they set out on their journey, we, too, begin this pilgrimage with a prayerful blessing.

Blessing

May this pilgrimage create in you a clear understanding of the Catholic Church story. May you go with a spirit of anticipation, and may you receive the new insights you hope for. May you see the hand of God and the guidance of the Holy Spirit in each age of the Church's history and in your own life, too. May you learn from the past and incorporate its valuable lessons into your own faith life. May you experience the joy and delight of those countless Christians who have dedicated their lives to bringing about God's reign on earth. May the peace of God be with you as you journey through the power of grace and prayer.

PART I

The Early Church

*From the First Century to the
Fall of Rome (A.D. 476)*

As preparation for your pilgrimage, spend some time reading the gospels and the Acts of the Apostles. Encounter anew this Jesus of Nazareth who is the most influential person in history. See his profound influence on his followers in the early Church through the power of the Holy Spirit.

We begin our pilgrimage in a remote village at the eastern end of the Mediterranean in Palestine, an area under Roman domination and ruled by Herod Antipas.

As we tread the streets of the hilly town of Nazareth, we encounter a young family of moderate means who live humbly and simply as devout Jews. They seem to be ordinary, and yet this is the environment in which Jesus, the promised Messiah and Son of God, grows up with Mary his mother and Joseph his foster father, a carpenter. We know little of Jesus in his growing years: he is born in Bethlehem between 6 B.C. and A.D. 6; he gets lost on a pilgrimage to Jerusalem (see Luke 2:41-52); and he lives in Nazareth of Galilee until he starts his public life, probably around A.D. 28 or 30. John, an itinerant preacher, baptizes Jesus in the Jordan river and singles out Jesus as the next prophet.

A small group of friends leave their livelihoods and families to accompany Jesus as he travels about preaching the Good News. For three years, Jesus goes about on his mission. He calls for repentance and faith. He proclaims the reign of God and reveals it in his healings: the lame walk, the blind see, and seekers discover one who makes a difference in their lives. Crowds gather everywhere, willing to pattern their lives on Jesus' message and example. Imagine Jesus' compassion and goodness as he speaks out for justice and concern for the poor.

Faith in Jesus as the Messiah does not come easily. Imagine how these early followers at times must question Jesus and wonder about his mission. Their faith keeps them loyal and steadfast, although they disturb the political leaders who are suspect of Jesus' intentions. They fear Jesus can cause upheaval and rob them of their power. The officials bring Jesus to trial, crucify him, and think they have thereby ended the threat to their control.

But Jesus' life and mission are not over. He rises from the dead, appears on various occasions, and after forty days, ascends into heaven. Jesus affirms his legacy with the commission of his followers: "Go therefore and make disciples of all nations" (Matthew 28:19). Though many details of Jesus' life are not known, what we do know we learn from the Gospels of Matthew, Mark, Luke, and John, which proclaim faith in Jesus. Suppose Jesus had lived, died, and risen from the dead, and no one noticed, what then? That would have been the end. But we know that's not the case.

Because Jesus is no longer physically present in this world, his grieving disciples gather for prayer in the upper room. Suddenly, the power of the Holy Spirit descends on the group as a strong wind blows outside and tongues of fire alight on each one. These once-fearful souls, convinced that Jesus truly is the promised Messiah, proclaim their faith in Jesus literally from the housetops. People from all over the Empire are able to understand the Good News in their native tongues.

Pentecost: The Birth of the Church

As Jews and outsiders of various nationalities and racial groups gather in Jerusalem for the Jewish pilgrimage feast of Shavuot (Pentecost), imagine how surprised you'd be to see the courage of these simple Galilean followers of Jesus and their mysterious ability to communicate with people in many different languages. Stand in amazement as you hear Peter recount the deeds of the man of Galilee whom the disciples believe is the Messiah. Witness the faith take root as the crowd of about three thousand hears, repents, and accepts baptism. Relive the dramatic scene—a motley group of seekers transformed into a community of faith. And so the Church comes into existence. Pentecost is truly the birthday of the Church.

Filled with even greater zeal, the disciples enthusiastically continue to proclaim the message of Jesus. They perform marvelous signs and miracles, proof that Jesus' mission continues through them. Although we have no documentation of the disciples' ministries, tradition teaches that they went out and evangelized the farthest ends of the then-known world. For example, Christians in India honor Thomas, whom they believe evangelized India.

These early believers live their faith in two ways—the Jewish way and the way of Jesus. Observe them go to synagogue, pray, and practice Jewish rituals and customs. Also join these early Christians on the first day of the week, Sunday, to commemorate Jesus' Resurrection. Pray with them and hear them recall the times spent with Jesus. Share a meal and partake of bread and wine as Jesus has bidden: "Do this in remembrance of me." These early Christians firmly believe Jesus lives on in their midst. See how their example of service, love, and common lifestyle draws many to follow the way of Jesus as they continue Jesus' mission. But notice too that their faith in Jesus conflicts with strict Jewish traditions. Gradually they abandon their Jewish ways.

One zealous young man, Stephen, eloquently witnesses to his belief in Jesus. His defense infuriates and angers the authorities, the Zealots. They stone Stephen, who becomes the first martyr of the young Church. Relive Stephen's faith and testimony in Acts 7:1-53.

Paul, Apostle to the Gentiles

We first meet Saul (later called Paul) as an avid persecutor of Christians at the stoning of Stephen. God redirects Paul's zeal to the Christian cause through a dramatic conversion experience, an encounter with the risen Lord, around A.D. 37. In extensive missionary journeys, Paul proclaims Jesus as the Messiah and establishes numerous faith communities throughout Asia Minor and Greece. Paul suffers martyrdom in Rome around A.D. 67. Because he spread the Christian message beyond the Jewish community to the whole Mediterranean world, Paul merits the title "Apostle to the Gentiles." Relive his life and mission recorded in the Acts of the Apostles, especially chapters 7-9 and 13-28. Capture his spirit and reflect on his understanding of Christ in Paul's epistles.

The early Christians, in their ardent commitment to Jesus, refuse to offer sacrifice and incense to the emperor. Because they gather for worship in secret, authorities suspect they are a subversive group plotting against the Empire. Early on, the Christians become a convenient target for persecution, first in A.D. 64, when Nero blames them for fires in Rome.

Persecution and Martyrdom

Though thousands of Christians give up their lives as martyrs in the ten major persecutions that last until the fourth century, the Empire does not succeed in snuffing out the Church. Christians become more adamant in their commitment. Church hagiography, the biographical accounts of the saints, tells of stories of the martyrs' unimaginable heroism and courage.

Ironically, the persecutions of Christians do not squelch their ideal but draw many to the faith, despite the possibility of martyrdom. According to tradition, all the apostles die as martyrs except John, who dies at a ripe old age in Ephesus, around A.D. 100.

By the end of the first century, the Christians are still the minority but continue to gain new members. Each local community meets for worship in private homes. Elders of the community, later called bishops, lead the service. Presbyters and deacons assist. The early Christians model their services and leadership structures on the Roman style of organization.

Oral Traditions Lead to the Writing of the Gospels

The biggest challenge for the first-century Church is to pass on the experience of Jesus when the first generation of Christians dies. See them gather in community, share memories, and tell stories of what Jesus said and did. Hear them relate details of his passion and death. They remember his healing miracles, teachings, and parables, and they relate stories of his birth and early life in Nazareth.

The early Christians proclaim these stories, experiences, and sayings of Jesus in the local communities. You know how it is when several people recount the same event. Although details may differ, basic features of the story remain the same. We see this pattern in the gospels as well. In each place where Christians meet, different versions of the Jesus story circulate among the believers, first oral and then written. The gospels of Matthew, Mark, Luke, and John emerge as the authoritative accounts because they originate from Christian communities closely associated with the apostles—Jerusalem, Rome, Antioch, and Ephesus.

Each gospel addresses people of varying backgrounds and presents a unique image of Jesus and his mission. The four gospels are not biographies, but proclamations of faith in Jesus.

Because a gospel passage is read at every Mass, you probably have some familiarity with the gospels. To get a fuller understanding of each gospel's take on Jesus, take time to read each gospel in its entirety. Notice how each evangelist portrays Jesus and his mission in a different way.

Mark, the earliest and shortest account, is written shortly after the persecution of Nero, between A.D. 65 and 70. As you read Mark, see a truly human Jesus with emotions and feelings, a Jesus in perpetual motion. Feel the impetuous nature of Peter. Note Jesus' deeds and his concise expressions, rather than lengthy discourses found in John, for example. Mark gives you the impression that Jesus is the activist, always doing, a Jesus engaged in round-the-clock activity. Mark relates details of Jesus' life from the public ministry until his Resurrection.

The Gospel of Matthew addresses Jewish Christians.

Jesus is the "new Moses," the fulfillment of the Old Covenant. Matthew says "as it is written in the Scriptures" many times to prove that Jesus fulfills the messianic prophecies. Matthew mentions customs familiar to Jews. Just like the Torah, the Hebrew Law (the first five books of the Bible), Matthew's Gospel is divided into five sections—the infancy, miracles, parables, teachings, and passion accounts. You hear a Jesus who truly speaks with authority. Sit on the hillside as Jesus proclaims his teachings in the Sermon on the Mount (Matthew 5-7). From your vantage point, you behold one who truly is "the new Moses."

In Luke you encounter a merciful and compassionate Jesus who heals the sick and welcomes outcasts and sinners. Luke alone relates the parable of the Prodigal Son and the story of Mary and Martha. Read Luke like a travelogue as Jesus moves from Galilee toward Jerusalem. Luke concludes his Gospel with Jesus' Ascension and continues the account of the early Church in the Acts of the Apostles.

Because the gospels of Matthew and Luke, written between A.D. 70 and 80, follow a pattern similar to Mark's, we refer to these three gospels as "synoptic," which in Greek means "to see things in the same way."

The Gospel of John transports you to another world. Written later than the other gospels, John's Gospel opens with the divine origin of Jesus: "In the beginning was the Word, and the Word was with God, and the Word was God" (John 1:1). John relates events of Jesus' life in a very symbolic and theological way.

In addition to the four gospels and the Acts of the Apostles, the New Testament includes fourteen letters that Paul is credited with writing to the Christian communities, seven pastoral letters of Peter, James, Jude, and

John, and the prophetic book of Revelation. These twenty-seven books, first listed in 367 by Athanasius, comprise the New Testament.

The Apostles' Creed

Imagine yourself as a fervent Christian in the early Church. Although the gospels and the epistles of Paul exist in written form, you know your faith mostly through what others tell you, because parchments and books are scarce. You long to express what you believe in a concise way. You remember some truths, but you cannot accurately state what you believe.

From the early second century, brief affirmations of the faith circulate among the Christians. Based on oral apostolic proclamations (like the one in Acts 2:22-39), easily memorized expressions of fundamental beliefs become a norm for baptisms and catechetical instruction in the early Church. Today we know one such expression as The Apostles' Creed. Although normally not used in liturgy today, it ranks as one of the major prayers of the Church. According to Saint Ambrose, we call it "The Apostles' Creed" because the twelve articles of faith are closely linked to apostolic teaching.

Apostolic Father and Apologists

We know about the ways in which the early Church celebrated liturgy and worship from other early writers. Their writings, though not considered Scripture, are significant for Christian self-understanding. We call Clement of Rome, Ignatius of Antioch, Polycarp, and others "the apostolic fathers" because their writings reflect authentic teaching from the apostles.

Other learned scholars and theologians of the early Church, called "apologists," explain and defend the faith in reasoned arguments and articulate Christian teaching through their writings:

Justin the martyr (100-165) argues that Christianity is the true religion.

Irenaeus (130-202) attacks heresy and organizes Christian teachings.

Clement (150-215), head of the catechetical school at Alexandria, and Origen (185-254) explain the faith in terms of Greek philosophy.

Tertullian (160-230) is the first major theologian to write in Latin and use the term *Trinity*.

You can learn more about the Church Fathers and apologists through the branch of theology called "patristics" or "patrology," which deals with early Christianity to about the fifth century.

Constantine and the Edict of Milan (313)

The reign of the Emperor Constantine marks a watershed in Christian history. Amid the political chaos engendered by several claimants vying for power, Constantine emerges victorious at the battle of the Milvian Bridge in 312. Convinced of Christianity's validity through a personal religious experience, Constantine grants religious freedom in the Edict of Milan (313). This ends periodic persecutions and puts Christianity on an equal footing with other religions. (Sixty-eight years later, the Emperor Theodosius proclaims Christianity the official religion of the empire and outlaws other religions.) Constantine enacts laws favoring Christians because his empire profits more if it recognizes Christianity. His laws set aside Sunday as a day of rest and enable Christians to worship openly. With increasing numbers of converts to Christianity, meeting in private homes becomes impractical. So Constantine builds churches and large public places—basilicas—for worship and community. Gradually Christians also take over the use of temples formerly used by other religions. The Pantheon in Rome, a museum today, is a former temple to all the Roman gods. Pope Boniface IV dedicates it as a Christian church in honor of Mary and All Saints on November 1, 609, All Saints' Day, which we still observe as a holy day.

Constantine also builds the basilica of Saint John Lateran, the cathedral church of Rome. He donates to the church his own residence, the Lateran Palace. (It becomes the papal residence of the bishop of Rome until 1309, when the pope moves to Avignon.)

Then Constantine, sole ruler of the Roman Empire, moves the imperial capital out of Rome to Byzantium, which he renames Constantinople. This shift to the East paves the way for greater rivalries between the Greek-speaking Church and the Latin-speaking Church, culminating in the East-West schism in 1054.

The Rite of Christian Initiation

After Emperor Constantine issues the Edict of Milan in favor of Christianity, many persons wish to become Christian. The Church has long had a formal process—called the "catechumenate"—by which people are initiated into the Christian faith community. Now, to distinguish between sincere seekers and those who request baptism for social advantages, the Church lengthens and intensifies this process of initiation. Through experiencing community and learning about the Good News, converts discern their call to the faith. This manner of receiving new members into the Church produces informed, transformed Christians. The culmination of the Rite of Initiation at the Easter Vigil welcomes catechumens into the Church as full-fledged Christians.

The catechumenate eventually falls out of use because the lengthy period of formation proves unmanageable with the large number of converts and the increase in infant baptisms. Not until the twentieth century is the catechumenate reinstated by the Second Vatican Council. Since 1988, the Rite of Christian Initiation (RCIA) is the norm parishes follow in the formation of new converts.

Picture yourself a baptized convert to Christianity in the fourth century. Through the catechumenate, you learn and experience the Christian way of life. You believe Jesus is the Messiah and fulfillment of the Hebrew prophecies. You hear the Good News and the stories of Jesus. You celebrate Jesus' presence in the sacred Word and in the Eucharist, and you gather for worship on Sunday with the community. You affirm your beliefs through the Creed, and you live a moral Christian life.

Understanding the Person of Christ and the Trinity: Heresies and Councils

As time goes on, you ask deeper questions about the nature of Jesus. How is Jesus related to God the Father? Who is the Holy Spirit, and what is the relationship with Father and Son? These questions may seem trite today. But how to express complex theological concepts and the mystery of faith in understandable terms is a challenge for fourth-century Christians and theologians.

If you listen to Arius (250-336), a priest of Alexandria, you are confused when he states that Jesus Christ is not equal to God. His thesis is soon hotly debated across the East. Some forms of Arianism continue to exist for several centuries. Because Constantine wishes to promote harmony, he calls the first ecumenical council in Nicaea in 325, which declares that Christ is one divine Person with two distinct natures, human and divine.

In 381 when Emperor Theodosius recognizes Christianity as the official religion of the Empire, he also calls the bishops together for the Council of Constantinople. They condemn Arianism again, and in answer to different opinions, they compose the Nicene-Constantinopolitan Creed. As the authoritative statement of Christian faith, the Nicene Creed today serves as the affirmation of faith at each Sunday liturgy.

You would think that the controversy and false ideas would come to an end. Not so. Another heretic, Nestorius, the patriarch of Constantinople, continues the discussion. If Christ is both divine and human, Mary can only be the mother of the human Jesus and not the mother of the Christ. The Council of Ephesus (431) condemns Nestorius and with Cyril of Alexandria proclaims Mary the "Theotokos," the God-bearer.

This declaration leads to another heresy, monophysitism, that Jesus Christ has only one divine nature rather than two distinct natures, divine and human. Pope Leo the Great brilliantly explains the nature of Christ as one divine person with two distinct natures, human and divine in a doctrinal letter on the Incarnation, which the bishops adopt as authoritative Christological teaching at the Council of Chalcedon in 451.

Beginnings of Monasticism   At the end of the third century, when Christians are no longer put to death for the faith, zealous souls seek a radical new way to follow Christ. Some decide they can "die for Christ" by "dying to self." Antony of Egypt (250) leads the way for the eremitic life, in which hermits devote themselves to prayer and sacrifice.

Pachomius (290-346) attracts many to an ascetic life, in which they live not as hermits but in community, the cenobitic way of life. Many monastic communities dot the Egyptian desert. These hermits and cenobites become models for contemplative religious life in the Church.

One of the most colorful figures of our first five hundred years is Jerome, monk and biblical scholar. As secretary to Pope Damasus in Rome, Jerome begins a Latin translation of the Bible. He uses the Greek version of the Hebrew Bible, the Septuagint, translated around 72 B.C., and the Greek New Testament. The Septuagint contains seven books not included in the Hebrew Bible—Judith, Esther, Tobit, Wisdom, Sirach, and the two books of Maccabees. Jerome's Latin translation is called the Vulgate, because it is in the people's ordinary (in Latin, *vulgaris)* language.

Jerome (340-420) and the Vulgate

As we near the end of the first leg of our pilgrimage, we meet one of the most significant personalities of the early Church—Augustine of Hippo. In his early life, he fathers a child, experiments with various lifestyles, and as an avid student of all philosophies, appropriates many exotic notions. His hedonistic lifestyle grieves his mother, Monica, a devout Christian. Ambrose, the bishop of Milan, influences Augustine, who makes a complete turnaround and by God's grace commits himself completely to Christ. As a fervent Christian, he uses his brilliant intellect to explain the faith.

Augustine of Hippo (354-430)

Subsequently Augustine becomes the bishop of Hippo in northern Africa, confronts heretics, and staunchly defends the faith. Augustine's legacy continues in his autobiography, *Confessions,* which relates his life and conversion experience, and in other famous writings, especially *City of God,* written after the sack of Rome in 410. He contrasts the worldly city to the heavenly city, in which God and good triumph.

The Roman Empire at the beginning of the fifth century is losing its integrity and power. People from the outskirts of the Empire take advantage of this weakened condition by infiltrating the Western Empire, even joining the Roman army and adopting Roman ways. First the Vandals invade northern Africa, and then the Huns target Rome. Later, the Goths, Lombards, and others come along.

The Church, now the lone stable authority in the West, exerts its influence. Pope Leo the Great confronts Attila the Hun in 452 and persuades him to leave Rome. Leo is not entirely successful, for the Vandals again show their power and ransack Rome a few years later. Leo convinces them neither to burn the city nor to massacre the people. But Rome cannot long withstand these onslaughts. In 476 the city of Rome falls totally into the hands of foreigners.

Of all leaders of the early Church, we need to pay particular attention to Pope Leo the Great, who not only dares the enemies of the Empire but also speaks out for papal primacy. Leo's reign, a challenging and crucial time, witnesses the disintegration of the Roman Empire in the West and theological controversies in the East. He devotes all his energy to preserving the unity of the Church and safeguarding theological correctness.

Although the Eastern churches argue that the patriarchs of the East have authority equal to that of the bishop of Rome, Leo upholds the primacy of the bishop of Rome based on Jesus' words in Scripture: "You are Peter" (Matthew 16:18a). Leo is the first pope to be buried in Saint Peter's in 461.

At the fall of Rome, the Church extends from northern Africa to the Euphrates, through Asia Minor and Syria to Europe as far north as Ireland. At the end of five centuries, two styles of Christianity emerge—East and West, Constantinople and Rome. They differ in language, rituals, theological emphases, and government but remain united as one Church. They share Scriptures, Creed, and official church teaching.

The Church in the West stands alone as the stable institution, with Rome as spiritual and civil center. The bishop of Rome assumes both political and spiritual leadership.

The Church in the East survives the fall of Rome and continues as an integral part of the Byzantine Empire. Ruled jointly by the emperor and the patriarchs of Constantinople, Antioch, Jerusalem, and Alexandria, the Church in the East extends into the Balkans, Asia Minor, Egypt, Syria, Palestine, and Mesopotamia.

THE EAST

What is it like to be a Christian in the Eastern part of the Empire in the sixth century? You look to the patriarch as head of the Church, and although you know the bishop of Rome is looked upon as the successor of Peter, you consider your patriarch and the bishop of Rome to be equals.

You are part of a Church that emphasizes theological and philosophical questions. You hear differing views as scholars continue to debate. The emperor has much to say regarding the Church, and attempts to settle matters peaceably.

You attend Divine Liturgy in churches decorated with colorful mosaics and icons. In Constantinople the Divine Liturgy is in the Greek language, while in other areas of the East, Christians might use their local language. There's something mystical and awesome about the service. Each gesture has profound meaning, and incense, processions, and candles help you sense the divine presence. Your married priest wears ornate garb similar to a Byzantine court official's dress. You receive leavened bread and wine as Eucharist. This is your way of worship, and you know that Christians in the Western Church in Rome worship differently.

THE WEST

As a Christian in the West at this time in history, you look for stability and peace. You also fear the Germanic tribes that threaten the once-powerful and unified Roman world.

Christianity is strange to these people, yet your bishops tolerate them, and they convert to the Christian way of life. The Church provides education and social services to all without discrimination, practical and organized in its efforts to evangelize the tribes.

Because entire tribes come into the Church en masse with little instruction, a different style of Christianity emerges in the West, one with vestiges of tribal customs adapted to Christian practices. The Mass follows a form, but the presider adapts the prayers to expressions tribal people can understand to make them feel welcome. Your church leaders follow the pattern of the Roman civil authorities. The bishop leads, with presbyters and deacons assisting him.

As you reflect on the story of the early Church, recall that the Church emerges from an insignificant group of disciples to an influential reality in its first five hundred years. Here are some treasures gleaned from contemplating these first five hundred years of the Church. You may have some of your own to add to the list.

CHRIST-CENTERED FAITH

The first Christians lived Jesus' teachings simply without complicated rituals. I admire the faith the early Christians show as they abandon former Jewish traditions and give their lives completely to Jesus, their model and example. The early Christians' Christ-centered faith inspires me to reflect on my priorities. Am I fully committed to Jesus? Is Jesus the center of my life and faith as he was for the first Christians? Does my life reveal the goodness and integrity of Christ who gives me guidance for living? Am I distracted by concern for externals rather than focusing my faith on Jesus?

EARLY CHRISTIAN WITNESS

As I read the New Testament, I am inspired by the love of early Christians for Christ and one another. As they huddle in the catacombs during the persecutions, secretly worshiping in memory of Jesus, what faith and determination they exhibit in the face of possible and even probable martyrdom. Do I possess that same feeling of concern and care for members of my faith community? Am I doing my share to make my local church and faith community as vibrant as that of the early Christians?

FREEDOM OF RELIGION

Little do I appreciate what it means to be able to attend church or practice my religion without outside interference. How would I react during persecution? If I were threatened with death, would I openly profess my faith in Jesus?

LOVE FOR SCRIPTURE

As I page through my Bible, how often do I think of those whose great labor and love of God brought Scripture into being? Am I fully aware of the great legacy of faith of the Hebrew Bible, our Old Testament? Each liturgy I hear the Word of the Lord. How can I appreciate more fully that the Lord really is speaking to me?

PROCLAIMING THE CREED

I owe a debt of gratitude to those who put the mysteries of our faith into words to help us more deeply understand our God. Do I recite the Nicene Creed with determined focus, reminding myself of the heritage the early theologians have left us?

MONASTIC PRAYER AND DISCIPLINE

I read accounts of the austere lives led by monks in the desert with great admiration. They live out in a radical way Jesus' invitation, "Come away to a deserted place all by yourselves and rest a while" (Mark 6:31a). Their prayer, solitude, and rigorous lifestyle encourage me to value and practice spiritual discipline in my life. In my busyness, do I set apart time to commune directly with God, do penance, and discipline my life? Do I follow the monks' example and open myself to a deeper relationship with God?

THE GRACE OF CONVERSION

It is not so much what Saint Paul and Saint Augustine did, but how their lives demonstrate the profound effects of the grace of God. Both men accomplish much, but only through the grace of God. Their lives are tales of how God can write straight with crooked lines. How can I respond more fully to God's promptings in my life?

UNITY IN DIVERSITY

Although I belong to the Roman rite, I need be aware that Christians of other rites also share our long tradition and history. Just as the rites of the Eastern Church have developed as specific expressions of particular cultures, so has my own Roman Catholic heritage. How can I become more appreciative of the diverse ways Roman and Eastern Christians exercise their faith?

PART II

The Early Middle Ages

From the Sixth Century to the Schism (A.D. 1054)

The second leg of our pilgrimage takes us through what some historians inaccurately label "the Dark Ages." But even our cursory survey of these five centuries proves them to be far from dark and non-productive. Experience the growth and struggles of the Church as it copes with the new challenges of mass conversions, missionary expansion, and theological tensions between East and West. Consider how the coming of Islam into the world impacts the religious scene.

A new worldview forms as Germanic invasions change the face of Western European civilization. The Latin language, though officially adopted by the Church, fades into disuse as the common tongue. Latin roots blend with expressions of various peoples and form the Romance languages.

Observe how the Church in the West, the sole political and religious power, organizes and expands its borders. The Church in the East, under the emperor's control, debates theological issues, develops its own liturgy, and eventually breaks with Rome.

Note how the Church, guided by the Holy Spirit, experiences rays of hope amid the chaos. Meet giants of faith, especially Pope Gregory the Great and Charlemagne, who stand out as individual catalysts of the faith. But we owe the Church's survival and success to the monasteries, which shape and preserve the faith of Western Europe during this period.

Monasteries: Preservers of the Faith

The monastic life of prayer and fasting is a total self-giving commitment to Christ. Monasteries, the anchors of spirituality both in the East and the West, become the chief repositories of spirituality, culture, and knowledge. Monks prize the tradition of the Church, pass on its teachings, and preserve classics, writings of the Fathers, and the Scriptures. Imagine what an arduous and time-consuming task was the creation of a single manuscript in the days before the printing press, each letter meticulously etched with indigo dye on papyrus or sheepskin. Monks spread the faith by their example and preaching.

Monasticism in the East concentrates on prayer, contemplation, and preservation of icons. Saint Basil (330-379), theologian and father of Eastern monasticism, founds monasteries in Asia Minor, present-day Turkey.

In the West, Italy and Ireland provide a solid bedrock of the faith, from which two distinct forms of monasticism and spirituality emerge—Benedictine and Celtic.

When we say "Irish," we instinctively think of Patrick *Celtic*
(389-460). We have images of Patrick preaching through- *Monasticism*
out the Emerald Isle ridding it of snakes and holding a
shamrock to explain the Trinity. As legendary as Patrick
tales might be, they pay tribute to one who plants the
faith firmly in Ireland, a Christian stronghold when
Anglo-Saxon barbarians invade Britain. Patrick finds Ireland to be fertile soil because the Christian message of hu-
mility and poverty appeals to the agrarian Irish character.

By 600 more than one hundred monasteries dot the
Irish countryside and serve as parish churches. Finnian
(549), the father of Irish monasticism, trains monks to
found monasteries. Because of Ireland's isolated loca-
tion, the Church develops quite independently, and Irish
monks develop a unique style of evangelization. See them
wander about the rural Irish countryside preaching appreciation of nature, a heroic asceticism, and simple
prayer. Celtic crosses are monuments to their influence.

View the artistic contributions of Irish monks in the
Book of Kells in Dublin and the Lindisfarne Gospels in
Durham. Be intrigued with their interest in your spiritual life. This soulfriendship with a spiritual mentor becomes a norm in their individual approach to spiritual
growth. The practice of private confession develops from
this approach, a more meaningful method than the hu-
miliating public confessions of previous centuries. This
manner of confessing sin becomes popular and spreads
rapidly. By the time of the Fourth Lateran Council in
1215, confession of sins to a priest becomes the norm
and still today is the method of the sacrament of reconciliation. The austere Irish monks emphasize penance
and sacrifice, and by the middle of the sixth century,
they evangelize Scotland and then head to the mainland
of northern Europe. Through the leadership of Columban

and Columbkille, monasteries flourish throughout Europe. But Irish monks and their spirituality meet rivals in the Benedictines, whose evangelical strategy differs.

Benedictine Spirituality

Meet Benedict of Nursia (480-547), a devout Italian who attracts followers to a prayerful, disciplined, communal lifestyle. Through a less austere and more practical spirituality than the Irish, Benedict advocates a balance of prayer, study, work, and rest in a simple practical rule. Monte Cassino, Benedict's monastery in southern Italy, becomes the hub for the numerous Benedictine monasteries throughout Europe.

Benedictine monks work among the peasants and develop agricultural methods, such as crop rotation. Unlike the individuality and mobility of the Irish monks, Benedict fosters a communal lifestyle and stability. Hundreds of Benedictine monasteries spring up throughout Europe during the Middle Ages. To this day, the Rule of Saint Benedict shapes the spirituality of many religious communities, and the Benedictine spirit inspires and influences the liturgical life of the Church. Many popes and bishops, trained as Benedictine monks, serve as examples of authentic spirituality in the Church.

POPE SAINT GREGORY THE GREAT (590-604)

Each age produces those giants of faith who provide leadership and direction in times of struggle. Meet Pope Gregory the Great, a Benedictine monk who, in the spirit of Saint Benedict, balances his administrative skills with a deep spirituality. Gregory negotiates with the Germanic invaders and integrates their customs with the Christian tradition, recognizing the creative potential of these peoples. Missionary interests extend northward and westward to France, England, and Spain.

Observe Gregory, who describes his mission as "servant of the servants of God," humbly dole out food and supplies during a famine.

While he acknowledges the political supremacy of the Byzantine Emperor in Constantinople, Gregory insists on the spiritual primacy of the Roman Church and the universal authority of the pope. He denounces the claim of equal power of the Byzantine religious leader.

Gregory continues the Benedictine spirit through his endorsement of celibacy and the development of the liturgy. He upholds Latin as the liturgical language and issues a ritual sacramentary. We call liturgical music "Gregorian chant" because Gregory takes interest in and compiles music for the Latin Church.

In 610 Mohammed, an Arabian youth in Mecca, has a **Islam** religious revelation through which he believes he is to preach the one God, Allah. Convinced of the sincerity of his calling, Mohammed forcibly and uncompromisingly preaches the message of "submission to Allah," which becomes the religion of Islam.

Because Mecca is the crossroads of commerce and trade, Mohammed possibly is acquainted with Christians and Jews. Along with Muslims, Mohammed considers Jews and Christians "people of the Book," with Abraham as common ancestor. The Qur'an (Koran), Islam's holy book, contains similarities to both the Old and New Testaments. Mohammed's dynamic and influential message appeals to nomadic peoples, so that at the time of his death in 632, all of the Arabian peninsula has adopted Islam, which soon spreads into northern Africa, Syria, Palestine, Egypt and Spain.

If not for the stamina and efforts of Charles Martel, who halts the Moors' advance into Gaul over the Pyrenees in 732, Europe too might be Muslim. Islam exists in Spain until Ferdinand and Isabella expel the Moors in 1492. A remnant of the Muslim occupation in Spain is evident in the unique architecture of Spanish churches.

Islam spreads eastward, and within a century, the Muslims have control of Syria, Palestine, and Egypt. Islam threatens the Byzantine Empire and totally overtakes it in 1453.

Conversion of the Franks

The Franks prove to be most beneficial to the Christian cause. The Frankish leader, Clovis, marries a Christian, converts to Christianity in 496, and thus causes the kingdom of France to become Christian. The most influential Frank, Charles Martel, in 732 overcomes the Islamic advance into France. This victory is decisive because Martel preserves the Christian religion for the West.

Charlemagne, Holy Roman Emperor (742-814)

Crowned emperor by Pope Leo III in 800, Charlemagne unites the Frankish empire into a single Christian state and advocates law and order. As patron of learning, Charlemagne places Alcuin in charge of the palace school, and his curriculum becomes a model and forerunner of the universities. Charlemagne also standardizes the liturgy and compiles a missal using the Gregorian sacramentary.

Feudalism

Charlemagne's reign and the dream of a unified Christian kingdom is short-lived. After his death in 814, Charlemagne's empire is divided into many principalities, each governed by individual lords. Without a central government, chaos and strife abound as nobles vie for territory and control. This situation leads to the political and social system of feudalism, which brings to Europe some peace and order at a time when trade and money are scarce. Under the feudal system, various levels of society emerge—nobles, clergy, warriors, and serfs.

Suppose you are living on the landed estate of a wealthy landowner or noble at this time. You receive lodging and security for your family. You in turn promise allegiance and military service to the owner. As a vassal to the lord, you pledge to protect him and if necessary go to war. You oversee serfs who work the land.

This feudal system greatly affects the faith. Because the Church and monasteries have much land, some bishops become lords of the estate, assume temporal leadership, and often lose sight of their spiritual role. Other bishops become vassals to the overlord, who controls Church affairs, even to the appointment of bishops and clergy. Such an arrangement leads to serious abuses.

Nepotism, the appointment of relatives and friends to clerical offices, diminishes the religious spirit. Those who pay for clerical appointments and privileges become guilty of simony. Lay investiture, the practice of secular rulers controlling church affairs and clerical appointments, threatens the Church and in time the Church loses its prestige and influence.

The papacy, too, suffers setbacks in feudal times. With all the separate kingdoms in Europe, the pope no longer provides unified support. Popes acquiesce to political ambitions of the nobility, and many of the popes from the ninth to the eleventh centuries have short reigns, meet violent deaths, or are ill-treated. When absolute monarchies assume power, feudalism disappears, and towns replace the nobles' landed estates. But a feudal hierarchy continues in the structure of Church administration into later centuries.

East-West Tensions   Feudalism affects the Church only in the West. The Church in the East remains part of the Byzantine Empire ruled by patriarchs and emperors and becomes more detached and separated from the Roman Church. Although a schism does not occur until the eleventh century, tensions increase during the early Middle Ages.

Papal authority is the biggest ecclesiastical issue leading to the schism. The Greeks acknowledge the bishop of Rome as successor to Peter and "first among equals," but they refuse to recognize that the pope has jurisdiction over both the East and the West. They look to their own patriarch as their leader.

Political tensions escalate when Charlemagne becomes the Holy Roman Emperor in 800, a rival to the Byzantine Emperor in the East. Serious strains deepen with two theological controversies—iconoclasm and the *filioque* clause.

Iconoclasm   Think of all the beautiful Church art that inspires you as you enter any Roman Catholic church. Do you realize that this art that we take so for granted is one cause of a split in the Church?

The controversy begins when in 717 Emperor Leo III bans the use of icons and images in churches because he believes that Christians are worshiping icons. He concludes that worshipers replace their devotion to God with exaltation of the physical icon to a divine status. Leo's iconoclasm forbids the use of images as idolatrous and in violation of the first commandment's warning against graven images. Monks who depend on the production of icons for a livelihood are persecuted and put to death during the iconoclasm controversy.

Saint John Damascene, a Syrian and doctor of the

Church, writes a potent defense of the veneration of icons. Pope Gregory II in Rome opposes the ban of images and supports the use of art that inspires and educates illiterate converts. The West considers images symbolic means to enhance devotion, but not adoration. The churches in Rome have statues, vestiges of enduring Roman influence.

The Second Council of Nicaea in 787 temporarily resolves the iconoclasm controversy when Empress Irene intervenes to restore the use of icons and clearly distinguishes between *worship* and *veneration.* But Emperor Leo V in 814 revives the argument, which lasts until 843, when Empress Theodora upholds the use of icons and ends the iconoclasm controversy. Orthodox Churches celebrate this event, the "victory of icons," on the first Sunday of Lent as the "Feast of Orthodoxy."

Another factor leading to the schism in 1054, the *filioque* controversy, may seem trite and only a question of semantics, but it has crucial consequences. Recall that the Nicene-Constantinopolitan Creed, compiled at the Council of Constantinople in 381, is accepted as the authoritative statement of Christian beliefs.

Filioque Controversy

However, the East and the West understand and explain the role of the Holy Spirit and the relationship to the Trinity with different theological emphases. The East stresses the unity of the Trinity and oneness of the divine essence in the Father: "The Holy Spirit proceeds from the Father *through* the Son." The West considers the Trinity as three equal distinct divine persons. The differences in these interpretations may seem inconsequential to us, but they have far-reaching implications.

The original form of the Creed at the Council of Constantinople states, "The Holy Spirit proceeds from the Father." At the Council of Toledo in 589, the Western

Church, to quell Arian heretical ideas (which deny the divinity of Christ), inserts the *filioque* clause into the Creed—"The Holy Spirit proceeds from the Father *and* the Son." *(Filioque* means "and the Son" in Latin.) The East considers this addition a tampering with the Creed. But the West asserts that the *filioque* phrase only represents a clarification, not an addition or alteration.

The *filioque,* part of the Roman Church's understanding, is popularized by Charlemagne in 810 in standardized liturgical books and is adapted by Rome in 1031.

The *filioque* still separates the East and the West. The Roman rites pray "The Holy Spirit proceeds from the Father and the Son," while Orthodox Churches pray "The Holy Spirit proceeds from the Father through the Son."

Pope Paul VI, when meeting with the patriarch of Constantinople in 1978, uses the Eastern version of the Creed in a joint prayer service, implying that the *filioque* does not affect essential Christian theology.

Today the *filioque* is not considered a roadblock to interfaith understanding. Next time you say the Nicene Creed at Sunday Mass, pay special attention to the phrase "proceeds from the Father and the Son" and remember how sincere theologians in times past argued over a seemingly trivial semantic matter because they wanted to present the faith accurately.

Immediate Causes of the Schism of 1054

In 867 Photius, a lay scholar, becomes patriarch of the East. Vehemently opposed to the Roman Church, he summons a synod and decries the supposed errors of the West, especially its stance on iconoclasm and the *filioque.* Pope Nicholas rejects the accusations and excommunicates Photius, who in turn excommunicates the Pope. This issue in due time is resolved but not forgotten as East-West tensions mount.

The climax occurs when Michael Cerularius, (1005-1059), the Patriarch of Constantinople, lists thirty-three grievances against the Roman Church and the pope. He also closes the Latin-rite churches in the East. Cerularius rejects the pope as head of the universal Church, clerical celibacy, the use of unleavened bread in the Eucharist, and the *filioque*. When Humbert, the papal legate, delivers a summons of excommunication, Cerularius mutually excommunicates the pope. The break is not definitive until a Latin Crusade sacks Constantinople in 1205. A final attempt to reconcile the churches at the Council of Florence in 1439 fails.

Efforts to mend the rift between the Roman and Orthodox Churches result in some Eastern Churches uniting with Rome under the authority of the pope. These "Eastern Catholic Churches," formerly "uniates," retain their allegiance to the pope and their own national identities, liturgies, customs, languages, patriarchs, and dioceses. Although rituals differ, Catholics may fulfill Mass obligation and receive sacraments in Eastern Catholic Churches united with Rome. Some Eastern Catholic Churches are the Byzantine, Greek, Melkite, Russian, Ruthenian, Serbian, and Ukrainian.

At the close of the eleventh century, the Roman Catholic Church stands alone in the West. The Church of the East, the Orthodox, closely allied with the emperor, continues its style of worship, liturgy, traditions, and cultural outlook until 1453 when the Ottoman Turks conquer Constantinople. The spiritual center of the Orthodox Church then moves to Moscow and continues after 1453 as the Russian Orthodox Patriarchate and other national churches with various rites.

The Church at the End of the First Millennium

I sift through the memories and impressions of this era and ask, What can I learn from this difficult time? How can I be a better Catholic by contemplating this part of Christian history?

DEDICATION OF MONKS

I realize the faith would not have spread throughout Europe without the efforts of devoted monks who traipsed over miles of foreign terrain to bring the faith to many people. I appreciate the precious manuscripts preserved by devoted monks bent over their tables, arduously copying the Scriptures and the classics. Think of those Irish monks and their innovative style of evangelization. As spiritual directors, they introduce private confession, which becomes so meaningful and popular that the Church adopts private confession as the manner in which to receive sacramental forgiveness.

INCORPORATION OF GERMANIC PEOPLES

At times we become so adverse to change that we do not see it as an opportunity for growth. We need to see an example in the flexibility of the Church in this period of history. The Church avoids putting obstacles in the way of the conversion of Germanic peoples by adapting their customs to Church teaching. Consider the observance of the date of Christmas, set at the winter solstice, parallel to the observance of the Saturnalia.

How challenging it must have been to bring these people into the Church! It helps me remember to see the good in those who do not appear to me to have potential. In accepting the Germanic peoples and adapting Christian rituals to fit their customs, the Church shows me that in this life there is always room for change and adaptation.

Appreciation of other cultures is so necessary today as so much information about other customs and cultures flashes before us on our TV screens. I appreciate the example of Pope John Paul II, who adapts to local customs as he travels around the world. He wears native ceremonial headgear, waves feathers, and enjoys the elaborate dances and ceremonies of Papua New Guinea.

THE VALUE OF LEARNING

The ability of early missionaries to explain the faith serves as an example for us to be committed to and conversant with the teachings of our faith. Can I intelligently discuss and instruct others on the basics of the faith? How confident am I when I am approached with questions about Catholicism?

ICONOCLASM

Though religious art was once a source of controversy, I can now appreciate beautiful art pieces and statues and marvel at the gift of human imagination and creativity. The iconoclasm issue helps me understand the differing opinions and viewpoints concerning the beauty and significance of art.

FILIOQUE

Each time I pray the Creed at Sunday liturgy, I remember how painstakingly theologians grappled with what our faith reveals and how to find the exact words to express that faith. I try to say the words "I believe in the Holy Spirit…who proceeds from the Father and the Son" with special devotion, realizing the pain and anguish of those who wrestled to find the right words. It affirms my faith in the mystery of the Trinity.

APPRECIATION OF OTHER RITES

I cannot look at the Great Schism in an altogether negative light. Although I bemoan the fact that Rome and the Orthodox are not united, I am enriched by attending Eastern Catholic services. I get goosebumps as I hear the polyphonic a cappella "Lord, Have Mercy" thundering at a Greek rite Mass.

Often we Roman Catholics think our rite is the only right rite. But looking at Church history, we realize that from earliest days various rites have been approved. Why not increase your experience by attending an Eastern rite Mass? If it is a Church united to Rome, you can validly receive the sacraments, including the Eucharist, even though it may take the form of leavened bread dipped in wine and received with a spoon.

PART III

The High Middle Ages to the Reformation

From the Eleventh Century to 1517

On the third leg of our pilgrimage, we encounter dramatic changes both in the world and in the Church. In the High Middle Ages, from the twelfth century to the sixteenth century, towns and an urban commercial society replace the feudal system. The Church is now split, and so when we speak of the Church from here on, we refer to the Western Roman Catholic Church. (The Orthodox East has its own history.) This is also an age of great strides in human endeavors, of spiritual giants, and of papal dominance. It is a time when the Church is at the apex of temporal greatness and at the same time a low point in morals. It is a time when laity realize their relationship with God can be enriched by other means besides the official services in the Church, a time of flourishing private devotions. As we read of how people live in those days, we marvel at the ingenuity and creativity they use in simple ways of life.

European civilization from the eleventh century parallels the story of the Roman Catholic Church. Some strong personalities take over the papacy. This era begins with a flourishing papacy, but it soon becomes a time of decadence and scandal.

Through all events, we marvel that the Holy Spirit preserves the Church. After each downfall and failure, the Church seems, like the legendary phoenix, to spring back with new life. The setbacks and obstacles of the Church during this era lead to greater fervor and spirituality in the next.

Cluny and Clairvaux   We begin this story with the monasteries as strongholds of the Catholic spirit. In 910 William of Aquitaine founds the monastery of Cluny, and to regulate the control of monastery property, he places it directly under papal control. Cluny soon becomes a centralized monastery with associate monasteries under it. It excels in elaborate and ceremonial liturgy, making it famous throughout Europe.

Noted for leadership and piety, monks of Cluny include popes and bishops, most notably Pope Gregory VII, Urban II, and Paschal II. The monasteries of Cluny dotting the European countryside flourish and become very wealthy. Monks amass landed estates and, while dedicated to the Lord, lead lives of wealth, ease, and comfort that soon require reform.

Desirous of a simpler lifestyle, some monks leave Cluny and found a monastery of reform at Citeaux in 1098. This Cistercian way professes simplicity, austerity, and poverty. The Cistercians prefer remote areas, and they work the fields to support themselves with products from their vineyards and farms.

Citeaux attracts a young spiritual searcher, Bernard (1090-1153), who arrives with a retinue of friends to lead the Cistercian life. In 1113 Bernard founds a second monastery at Clairvaux, and soon many Cistercian monasteries appear throughout Europe. Their strict way of life influences many, and soon Cistercians become a model for contemplative communities. Bernard of Clairvaux proves to be one of the bright lights of the Middle Ages. Dante so admires Bernard that in the *Divine Comedy* Bernard stands as greeter at the heavenly gate. Among the saintly leaders of the Middle Ages, Bernard of Clairvaux holds a prominent place.

Crusades (1095-1290)

We arrive at a time in our Catholic Church story that we would like to forget, a time of "holy war" and the pillaging of innocents. The Crusaders, although motivated with fervent faith and zeal, accomplish their ends with violence and destruction. They aim to conquer the Holy Land, but they ruin everything in their path.

In the Middle Ages, pilgrimages are popular ways to respect the memory of sacred places and to gain spiritual merit. The Christians of Western Europe highly prize the places where Jesus lived, and so as an act of devotion, they undertake arduous pilgrimages to Palestine—the Holy Land.

However, Christians find it increasingly difficult to make pilgrimages peacefully, since the Muslims control the Holy Land. Likewise, the Muslims have their eyes on the Byzantine Empire and Constantinople. The Byzantine emperor asks Pope Urban II for aid in ridding the area of Muslim control. To marshal troops to enter battle for the cause, the Church promises complete remission of sins in return for service in the Crusades. Anyone who dies in the noble pursuit is guaranteed direct entry into heaven. These spiritual promises—indulgences—are not the only motivation. Young soldiers join the Crusades for adventure, others seek freedom and monetary gain, while others find the Crusades an opportunity for spiritual growth. Whatever their motives, myriads of young warriors sign up in the Crusades, convinced of a noble purpose. The Crusades are so called because of the cross (in Latin, *crux)* embroidered on the crusaders' garb. They begin as fervent pilgrimages and turn into military expeditions when the pilgrims' aims are thwarted. Accounts of the crusaders' endeavors read like logs of war plans and strategies. Overzealous Christians fight their way through, regardless of who stands in the way.

When you consider the Crusades think not only of war and havoc. Yes, that was part of it and the injustices committed in the name of religion are skeletons in the closet of our Catholic Church story.

The eight Crusades from 1095 to about 1270 do not reach their primary goal of permanently conquering the Holy Land. But the Crusades have a compelling effect on Europe for years to come. The Crusades open the door to the other side of the world, hitherto unknown to the West. Europe enters an era of developing towns and burgeoning trade and commerce. The Crusades widen the horizons of Western civilization. The world expands beyond current Western notions.

The Papacy   The papacy declines in power and prestige because corrupt and weak pontiffs in the eighth and ninth centuries concede to secular rulers. King Henry III (1017-1056) of the German Holy Roman Empire installs a series of German popes who continue to practice simony and nepotism.

Pope Nicholas II (1058-1061) takes the lead in ridding the papacy of lay interference. In 1059 he issues a decree that only the college of cardinals may select the pope and not secular rulers. This tradition continues to this day.

Pope Gregory VII (1073-1085) works for Church independence and supremacy. In 1075 he issues a decree outlawing the appointment of religious leaders by secular rulers. He calls for a more consistent enforcement of clerical celibacy and affirms papal infallibility, which becomes dogma in the nineteenth century. But his reform efforts cost him dearly. His ideas conflict with King Henry IV who assigns an anti-pope. Cardinals and bishops in Rome side with Henry. They rise against Gregory who finds haven in a monastery and dies in exile.

Gregory is a precursor of another reformer, the most influential pope of the Middle Ages, Pope Innocent III (1198-1216). Through his administrative skill, he exercises control over the papal states, the Church, and Western Europe. He governs the Church during two crusades and develops the hierarchical structure of authority—pope, cardinals, bishops, and clergy. He lays the cornerstone for centralization of Church powers, a model for succeeding generations. As an ardent defender of the faith, Innocent III commissions the Dominicans to ward off the Albigensian heresy.

But we remember Innocent III most for the Fourth Lateran Council in 1215 at which he issues many decrees concerning the number of the sacraments, the definition of the Real Presence, and regulations regarding reception of penance and Eucharist.

Innocent's legacy is blighted by his ruthless reform

attempts to search out heretics by the Inquisition. He requires Jews and Muslims to wear a special badge, an outrage for which Pope John Paul II recently asked forgiveness.

The Mendicants

Imagine how the face of Europe is changing. Towns and cities spring up. Populations shift more from rural to urban areas. Clustered together in narrow streets and crowded into close quarters, people come more into close contact with others, and lifestyles change.

The Church becomes the focal point in town and the center of religious and social life. People engage in trade, commerce, and cottage industries.

This closeness to the people requires a new type of ministry and outreach. No longer is it feasible for monks to remain cloistered and isolated in their rural monasteries. A new form of religious life evolves. The mendicants, especially the Franciscans and Dominicans, depend on alms and minister among the people.

THE FRANCISCANS

You are familiar with the humble friar, Francis of Assisi. Born in 1182 as Giovanni Bernardone, we know him by his nickname, "Francis" (The Little Frenchman), because of his stylishness and love of fine clothes. During an illness he undergoes a spiritual transformation and vows to follow Christ in a simple life and spirit of poverty. Through his preaching, he soon attracts many to follow as he rebuilds the church of San Damiano, a symbol of the rebuilding of the whole Church. Francis's love of nature and creation makes him the patron of animal lovers. He travels to the Holy Land and witnesses a skirmish in 1219 during the Crusades. His humble mien so impresses the sultan that he allows Christians to visit the

Holy Land. The Franciscans become known throughout the world.

Clare of Assisi (1194-1253) joins Francis and founds the Poor Clares, a contemplative order for women devoted to prayer and penance.

THE DOMINICANS

When the Albigensian heretics pose a threat to the Church, Pope Innocent III calls on a Spaniard, Dominic Guzman (1170-1221), to preach and argue theology with the heretics. Albigensianism rejects the goodness of creation, the humanity of Christ, and the sacraments. Because the heretics live a strict life, they cause confusion to devout Catholics. To quell the heresy, Dominic and his followers form a new order, the Order of Preachers, the Dominicans. They emphasize the study of theology and preaching the faith.

Dominic's love of Mary prompts the spread of devotion to the rosary through the preaching of Dominican friars.

Cathedrals

As you stand in awe before the massive cathedrals built in the Middle Ages, you marvel at the ingenuity and labor involved. The cathedrals of Notre Dame in Paris, Chartres, and Cologne stand as witnesses to the faith. Consider the labor of many workers spending backbreaking hours in hauling massive boulders from the mountainside. Crane your neck, and peer skyward to the top of the cathedral. The structure draws you closer to the spiritual world it symbolizes. The medieval cathedrals are truly marvels of faith and the human spirit.

The Gothic cathedral spires dominating the skyline of many medieval cities prove staunch witnesses to the faith. Built when piety expresses itself in tangible signs, cathedrals become for the laity the symbol of their beliefs. Stained glass windows, the "bibles of the poor," portray the Christian mysteries in brilliant, luminous color.

Education   In the Middle Ages, only clerics and nobles receive any formal education. Those skilled in the arts or handiwork come under the aegis of a master. They learn the trade and work as apprentices until skilled enough to work on their own.

Most monastic communities, adept at farming, earn their livelihoods with crops as income. As civilization shifts from rural areas to urban centers in the twelfth and thirteenth centuries, artisans and craftsmen gather in towns.

Under papal auspices, scholars and students form guilds and unions to protect their rights. The university becomes the center of learning, specializing in advanced education in theology, philosophy, science, classics, and rhetoric. Most noteworthy of the large universities are Bologna, Paris, and Oxford.

The works of Aristotle, at first considered a threat to Christian beliefs, come to be seen as aids in understanding the faith. Theological truths joined with philosophers' reasoning explain the Christian mysteries. This organizing of Catholic truths with concepts of Greek philosophy, called scholasticism, becomes the endorsed method for theological training.

THOMAS AQUINAS

A young Dominican student, Thomas Aquinas (1225-1274), believes wholeheartedly that our human senses can help toward a deeper spirituality and faith. He works out a whole theology showing how our faith can be explained in the light of human reason. The result of his work is the *Summa theologica,* a monumental synthesis of Catholic belief. Over time, Aquinas's genius is recognized, and the *Summa* becomes a standard text of theological studies. We consider Aquinas as the greatest theologian of the Middle Ages, just as Augustine of Hippo is for the early Church.

The papacy in the fourteenth century begins with pomp and splendor as Boniface VIII (1294-1303) declares 1300 a Holy Year and blesses the Jubilee Doors, a custom still observed. But Italy is torn apart by feuds and instability. In 1305, with no agreement on the papal successor, a Frenchman, Clement V (1305-1314), accepts the papacy to flatter France's Philip IV. Clement never reaches Rome, but takes up residence in a Dominican monastery in Avignon.

The Avignon Papacies (1308-1377)

From 1308-1377, seven French popes settle in southern France in Avignon, which becomes a commercial mecca for bankers, artists, and scholars, as well as a city of papal luxury. The Avignon popes flourish in wealth and ease. As astute administrators of financial affairs, they thrive by imposing heavy taxes on the clergy.

Not until 1377 does the pope, Gregory XI (1370-1378), return to Rome, at the urging of Catherine of Siena. Violence breaks out, and he soon dies. The papal question is far from being resolved, and greater problems loom on the horizon.

You would think that with the pope's return to Rome all would get back to normal. But the papal move back to Rome inflames the ire of the French. After Gregory XI, the conclave elects Italian Urban VI, who turns out to be harsh, intemperate, impudent, and hated by many. Catherine of Siena chides him to mend his ways, but he continues his papacy until 1389, when he is poisoned.

The Great Western Schism (1378 - 1417)

To show disapproval of Urban's election, a cortege of French cardinals returns to Avignon in 1378, and believing Urban's election invalid, they elect Clement VII as an Avignon pope.

So now that the Church has two popes, Italian and French, each believes he is the rightful pontiff, and so they excommunicate each other. How divided is the Church! To whom should allegiance be given? Some countries side with Rome and Urban, and others look to French Clement VII as pope. Imagine the papal expenses—two curias, two colleges of cardinals, two centers of administration.

Catholics wonder who is the rightful pope. In 1409, when Gregory XII is pope in Rome and Benedict XIII is "pope" in Avignon, a council is called in Pisa. However, this decision makes matters worse. The council elects a third pope, Alexander V, who soon is succeeded by John XXIII (1410-1414). Yes, this is the same name as that of the Vatican II pontiff, who in taking the name, subtly implies the invalid papacy of the first John XXIII.

The Council of Constance (1414-1418) finally solves the multi-pope dilemma. Gregory XIII abdicates, John XXIII resigns, the Avignon Benedict XIII is deposed, and a rightful pope is chosen, Martin V (1417-1431), who restores papal unity. But the prestige of the papacy suffers for decades to come. Scandals, immorality, nepotism, simony, and concubinage escalate within the papacy.

Today we take for granted that one pope resides in Rome, but as we consider the struggles of the Middle Ages, we appreciate the stability and spiritual leadership of the popes of our time.

Imagine yourself as a Catholic in the Middle Ages, the Age of Faith. While the Church struggles through difficulties, you as a lay person practice a deep simple faith, unaware of the scandals in the Church at higher levels. Your Catholic faith and life centers on the parish church as the hub of all social, educational, and cultural activities.

You look forward to Mass on Sundays when villagers come into town and bring their goods for the market in the square. You attend the Latin Mass celebrated by your parish priest and adore Jesus in the host when it is raised. You watch as a silent observer and do not receive Communion, which is only for special occasions. The Mass is simple, and except for the sermon, you do not understand the language. But your faith tells you something very special occurs—Jesus is present here. After Mass, everyone joins for lunch and visits the market.

The parish priest, trained at the cathedral school, not only says Mass, baptizes, marries, and buries, but he also visits the sick and prisoners, feeds the poor, and is the arbiter in village squabbles.

You acquire skill as a craft apprentice from a master tradesman. You learn about God at home and also from the priest who gathers townsfolk together to tell Bible stories. You like to look at the illustrated manuscript he received from the monastery outside of town.

You look forward to feastdays when you go into the big city for Mass at the cathedral, a respite from the humdrum daily routine. As you admire the pointed cathedral spires that reach like folded hands into the sky, you feel so small. Dwarfed by the huge interior, you gape in wonder as the sun glistens through the figures of Bible characters and saints on stained glass windows. The bishop, garbed in gold vestments, leads the procession. Glorious music and incense add to the pageantry.

You watch the Bible stories come to life as actors and mimes use their talents to dramatize gospel scenes in a mystery or miracle play.

As the priest elevates the host at the consecration, church bells ring, and you adore Jesus present on the altar. Christ for you is God in human form. So you love to hear stories of his birth, life, and passion. You look forward to Christmas when the nativity story comes alive with the crèche, a custom started by Francis of Assisi. Since you cannot go to the Holy Land and walk in the footsteps of Jesus, you follow Jesus in his passion through the pictures on the wall of the church, the Stations of the Cross. You believe that you receive the same graces for this act as you would had you gone on pilgrimage, for which you can gain an indulgence.

Since you cannot read, you rely on your memory and learn your prayers by heart. You know the Our Father, Hail Mary, Glory Be, and Creed. How happy you are when a Dominican friar teaches you how to combine thinking of Jesus' life and honoring Mary in prayer through the rosary.

At times the priest displays a relic, some memento of a saint or martyr. You reverently kiss it and say a prayer, hoping that the saint can help you. You know you cannot buy a relic, but in your room you have a corner set apart for a memento of a holy village woman who has died. When people pray to her, sometimes someone gets well. Although your village honors her as a holy person, you cannot call her "saint." Since the faithful honor so many holy people, Pope Gregory IX in 1234 decrees that you honor holy people only if the pope canonizes them.

Since a third of the population dies in the Black Death (1347-1350), you pay more attention to death and what lies beyond life. You live your faith in your daily life by praying and doing good to all. You try to live well so that one day you will go to heaven. When you commit sin, you go to the priest who gives you absolution in confession. You realize that the Church is important to you and that Jesus' mission continues through the priests, bishops, and pope in Rome.

The faith of the ordinary person in the Middle Ages is simple and attuned to the spiritual in everyday life. Mystics experience God in extraordinary ways through contemplation. They develop a deep relationship with God through intense love and knowledge of God. Some mystics of the Middle Ages live the interior life at such a deep level that often, so wrapped up in God and the spiritual world, they experience visions and other spiritual phenomena. Mystics aspire to holiness, and often their writings contain details of what God reveals to them. Let us meet some who contribute much to the spiritual heritage of the Church.

Mystics and Saints

CATHERINE OF SIENA (1347-1380)

Catherine of Siena, the twenty-third child in the family of a textile merchant in Siena, spends her life praying and caring for the sick as a third-order Dominican. As a mystic, she develops an intense personal relationship with God and becomes a model for others who look to her for guidance and direction. In her deep concern for the Church and the desire to restore spiritual discipline and unity to the Church, Catherine travels to Avignon to encourage the pope to return to Rome, which he does in 1378. She advises Urban VI in 1379 to soften his arrogance, and she sends letters to rulers and bishops to support the pope in the return to Rome. Her courage and spirituality earn for her a prominent place in Church history as a Doctor of the Church.

HILDEGARD OF BINGEN (1098-1179)

At an early age, Hildegard enters the convent, where she uses her gifts of intelligence and love of God in a remarkable way. She excels in medical expertise as a physician and uses her musical skills as a composer. But we remember Hildegard mostly for her theological understanding and deep spirituality. As mystic, abbess, and confidante of Bernard of Clairvaux, Hildegard lives on in accounts of spirituality and in her vivid descriptions of mystical visions. Today we consider Hildegard one of the great spiritual masters of the Middle Ages.

THOMAS À KEMPIS (1380-1471)

Monk, spiritual writer, and member of the Brethren of the Common Life, we know Thomas through his classic work *The Imitation of Christ,* a practical manual of spiritual guidance.

JULIAN OF NORWICH (1342-1413)

English mystic and recluse, Julian addresses the problem of reconciling the existence of evil with God's loving concern. In *Revelations of Divine Love,* Julian describes her visions and her conversations with Christ.

THE CLOUD OF UNKNOWING

An unknown English mystic uses a different approach to describe spiritual experiences in *The Cloud of Unknowing.* God cannot be known through images and concepts but only by desire in wordless prayer and silence. True spiritual understanding happens when God pierces through the cloud that obscures the divine. This volume is one of our great spiritual classics.

We now come to one of the most intriguing eras of our Catholic Church story—the Renaissance. This period of cultural rebirth from the 1300s to the 1600s was one of renewed interest in ancient Roman and Greek classics and a sudden upsurge of new inventions, discoveries, scientific advancements, and all forms of human art and creativity.

The Renaissance: Rebirth of Culture and the Arts

The Renaissance primarily begins with an attitude, a state of mind. People look at life differently and enjoy the good things the world offers. The human being is considered to be not just God's creation but endowed with gifts and talents to make life better. Possibly this shift comes about when, in the aftermath of the Black Plague, people again appreciate the gift of life and human dignity. Interest in the material world replaces human preoccupation with the spiritual.

Rapid change in our present day prepares us to imagine what effects the Renaissance has on medieval life. The Crusaders introduce into the West exotic treasures of the East. Cities spring up and trade increases. Merchants, craftsmen, artists, and scholars become enthused and find outlets for their creative endeavors. The names of Michelangelo, Raphael, and DaVinci dominate the Renaissance scene. We still reap the benefits of the beauty and culture of Renaissance days.

The invention of the printing press by Gutenberg in 1449 encourages literacy and publishing. Daring seafarers open Europe to the other side of the ocean. Portuguese and Spanish explorers lead the way, especially Columbus, DeSoto, Magellan, and Vasco De Gama.

But the people of the Renaissance do not ignore the

spiritual entirely. If you want to know how they imagine the afterlife, delve into Dante Alighieri's *Divine Comedy.* Written in Italian, the *Divine Comedy* introduces you to historical persons and their destiny in the afterlife. Travel with Dante as Virgil guides him through hell, purgatory, and heaven. Stand at the heavenly gates and join in the angels' glory. Dante's vivid imagery of the afterlife really brings to life the unseen mysteries. Dante gives us an inspiring and vivid glimpse of the spiritual world, but he also makes serious commentary on the evils of his day and the flaws of people in power.

The Renais-
sance Popes

The popes of the Renaissance are caught up in the excitement of the Renaissance. They concentrate on temporal concerns and heartily welcome the cultural revival. Rome becomes the center of art and culture. Though they are more worldly than holy, the ten Renaissance popes leave their mark on the Church as patrons of artistic endeavors and of the great Renaissance artists.

But other concerns also demand their attention. They need to keep control of the Papal States, which at this time comprise much of central Italy. With the fall of Constantinople in 1453, the Ottoman Turks pose a threat to the European mainland, and the Renaissance popes often call for a Crusade against the invaders. To keep peace and maintain their authority, the popes enter compromising alliances with neighboring kingdoms.

Because all this requires revenue, the popes resort to fund raising, often by devious, scandalous, and abusive means. They sell indulgences, accept bribes for clerical offices, and impose exorbitant taxes. The popes promote improvements and new buildings in Rome to attract pilgrims in hopes of raising the Roman economy. They appoint relatives to the privileged status of cardinal and pope. Several Renaissance popes are nephews of other popes.

Of the ten Renaissance popes, from after the Western Schism to the Reformation, some merit specific mention.

SIXTUS IV

Sixtus IV (1471-1484), a Franciscan friar, proves to be a true Renaissance man. He transforms the face of Rome, beautifying the city and streets. He commissions the beautiful Sistine Chapel and the Ponte Sisto, a bridge over the Tiber, both of which bear his name. He builds a hospital and organizes the world-famous Sistine choir. To quell heretics, Sixtus authorizes Ferdinand and Isabella to carry out the Spanish Inquisition.

ALEXANDER VI

Alexander VI (1492-1503), of the Spanish Borgia family, leaves a major blot on papal history, fathering illegitimate children. But we remember Alexander VI in another respect. In 1492 when Spain and Portugal vie for supremacy in explorations into the New World, Alexander VI settles the dispute by placing the Line of Demarcation through the Azores on a map. The lands west of that marking are Spanish claims and Portugal controls lands east of the Demarcation Line. Clearly the pontiff favors Spain. This explains why Brazil speaks Portuguese while the rest of Latin America speaks Spanish.

JULIUS II

Julius II (1503 -1513), nephew of Sixtus IV, known for his warrior skills, goes to war to recapture papal territory. His military concern leads him to implore the Swiss for protection of Rome and the pope. Since then the Swiss Guards provide official protection to the pope.

As a staunch supporter of the arts, Julius commissions Bramante, Michelangelo, and Raphael to work on Saint Peter's and other Vatican chapels.

Leo X

Leo X (1513-1521), of the Medici family, who becomes a cardinal at age thirteen and pope through bribery, brings the Renaissance era to an end. He exhausts the papal treasury by his extravagant lifestyle and pompous ceremonies along with excessive expenses to build Saint Peter's Basilica. To support the project, Leo embarks on a massive campaign to sell indulgences. Oblivious to the widespread cry for reform, Leo continues in his lavish ways. Ignoring Luther's specific challenge to debate, Leo excommunicates Luther and thus begins the Reformation, a sad chapter in our Catholic Church story.

The Renaissance bequeaths magnificent art treasures to the Church, yet the Church itself desperately needs spiritual reform and renewal. The Church at the beginning of the sixteenth century has lost its spiritual prestige and, like other worldly, institutions is run as a business enterprise. A Reformation is not only inevitable, but it is necessary for renewal.

Forerunners of the Reformation

The reformers, critical of the Church's wealth and clerical immorality, are not godless church-haters but begin in a spirit of sincere desire for change. They believe the rituals, dogmas, and cults of the saints obscure the authentic Christian message about Jesus Christ. So reformers appeal to the authority of the Bible and call for inner renewal.

The reformers are well-meaning, but the manner in which they make known their concerns leads to conflict and ultimately a breaking away from the Roman Church.

Although Martin Luther triggers the Reformation, the process of reform begins earlier with those who attempt to correct abuses and dare to suggest changes.

JOHN WYCLIFFE

John Wycliffe (1324-1384), an English priest, preaches against flagrant abuses in the Curia and calls for a return to the simple lifestyle of the early Christians. He organizes bands of itinerant preachers, the Lollards, and translates the Bible into English. Many years after Wycliffe's death, the Council of Constance in 1415 condemns his actions and exhumes and burns his remains.

JOHN HUSS

John Huss (1369-1415), a priest professor in Prague, agrees with Wycliffe and also calls for reform. Because Huss denounces the papacy, he is charged with heresy. The Council of Constance in 1415 burns him at the stake. The followers of Huss in Bohemia war against Catholics, model their lives on Huss's ideals, and form the Moravian Church.

ERASMUS

Desiderius Erasmus (1466-1536), a Dutch humanist writer, attacks corruption in the Church in a popular satire, *In Praise of Folly,* which heightens belligerence toward the Church.

You would think that these attempts at reform would bring about some good effect. Rather they lead to even stronger animosity toward the Church. Though individual charismatic leaders lead efforts of reform that fail, the Church continues in its decadent state—until Martin Luther arrives on the scene and the Reformation begins in earnest.

Suppose you, a Catholic, live in a German village at the start of the sixteenth century. You are faithful to the Church and the pope, even though you realize many clergy are not living according to their calling. God for you is a harsh judge who will punish you severely for your wrongdoings. You fear the fires of hell and purgatory. So you do everything your religion demands and pray you will go to heaven.

As you leave church one day, you meet a Dominican friar, John Tetzel, who tells you that all your sins and temporal punishment will be taken away if you put coins into his coffer to help build the basilica in Rome. You give and believe your generosity frees you from God's wrath. You wonder if it's true that authorities use the money for other purposes. The Church seems unfair. The poor people must donate money while the clergy live lives of ease. Most people are angry with the Church and are powerless to do anything to correct the situation.

As you walk through Wittenberg in 1517, you notice ninety-five theses tacked to the cathedral door. The Augustinian priest, Martin Luther, is angry with the Church, and he challenges anyone to debate the issues. Instead of debating, Church officials summon Luther. Meanwhile he distributes leaflets, which cause an uproar all over the country and beyond. Little do you realize that you are part of an upheaval that will affect the Church and the world for centuries to come—the Protestant Reformation.

Martin
Luther
(1483-
1546)

Although Luther means well and does not intend to start a new Church, his actions mushroom into blatant hostility toward the Church. Luther refuses to recant his statements and bases his objections on justification by faith alone. He disavows any need for rituals and customary traditions of the Church. An avid Scripture scholar and linguist, Luther utilizes the new printing press invention to disseminate his ideas with pamphlets and publications that reach far beyond his own land. The Church condemns Luther's ideas as heresy and excommunicates him. The nobles who support Luther provide him protective custody at Wartburg, where he translates the Bible into German.

The ordinary layperson finds comfort in and welcomes Luther's ideas at a time when dissatisfaction for the Church is rampant. Rioting crowds demand justice and protest the abuses and practices of the Church. War breaks out between opposing factions. The dissenters break from the Church and become the Lutheran Church. Luther's actions extend into other countries and others call for reform.

ULRICH ZWINGLI

Calvinist Reformers

Ulrich Zwingli (1484-1531), a priest in Switzerland, likewise feels the need for the Church's reform, though he disagrees with Luther on several theological points. Zwingli leads his followers to war against Catholic Swiss cantons who do not accept his teachings. He dies in the battle.

JOHN CALVIN

John Calvin (1509-1564), a French lawyer, rigorously picks up Zwingli's principles and works for reform. He organizes the reformation in Geneva, Switzerland, establishes a theological college, and is influential in his radical theology. He believes God determines who is saved and that humans can do nothing on their own to attain salvation. This theory of predestination and

Calvinism take hold in the Netherlands, Prussia, the Palatinate, and France, where Calvinists are known as Huguenots.

JOHN KNOX

John Knox (1513-1572), a Scottish priest, adopts Calvin's ideas and spreads the reformed religion to Scotland, England, and the New World. Followers of Calvin and Knox are known as Presbyterians. Puritans who emigrate to America and follow Calvin's theology become known as Congregationalists.

Henry VIII (1509-1547) and the Church of England (Anglicans)

The Reformation enters England not because of doctrinal or theological issues but because of King Henry VIII's personal problems. In 1534 he requests the pope's permission to divorce Queen Catherine of Aragon so he can marry Anne Boleyn. The request denied, Henry rebels, is excommunicated, and proclaims himself the head of the Church of England. Saints Thomas More and John Fisher, who try to dissuade Henry, are beheaded.

Henry does not deny doctrinal truths and retains many of the Roman Catholic externals and liturgy. He rejects the authority of the pope and closes monasteries.

This is the beginning of the Anglican Church, which is today the official church of England. The monarch of England is the head and the Archbishop of Canterbury is chief prelate.

Anglican settlers in Virginia wish to break all ties with England when America becomes independent in 1790, and they become known as Episcopalians. During the Industrial Revolution, John and Charles Wesley wish to minister more effectively to the working classes and form the Methodist Church.

Some reformers, the Anabaptists, believe in a radical strict observance of Christian ideals. They reject rituals and ceremony, baptize only adults, preach separation from the world, refuse to carry arms, and live a simple communal lifestyle. The Hutterites, Amish, Mennonites, and Quakers survive as offshoots of these radical reformers.

Radical Reformers: The Anabaptists

The many denominations of Protestant Christianity develop from these four reform groups—Lutherans, Calvinists, Anglicans, and Anabaptists.

As I try to garner insights and lessons that can help me in my spiritual life today, I am filled with mixed emotions. At times I am proud of the Church and at other times filled with shame. I marvel how the Church survives the tumultuous era from the eleventh to the sixteenth century. The Church reaches the height of worldly prestige and yet sinks to its lowest ebb.

Reflecting on the Third Five Hundred Years

THE CRUSADES

The Crusades conjure up images of knights and kings marching valiantly to fight for the Lord. I admire the zeal and courage of the crusaders in their attempt to save the holy places. What faith to leave all for the sake of Christ and knowing one might not return!

But I feel ashamed as I read accounts of the crusaders' exploits and the violence they use to achieve their goal. I decry their methods and feel remorse for the innocent who die because they are in the way of crusaders' ambitious plans. This truly is an era I would like to blot out from our history. I resolve to recognize and respect all religions.

Four Main Protestant Reform Movements

Lutheranism (1517)

MARTIN LUTHER
Germany
Lutheran churches • Pietist movement

Calvinism (1521)

JOHN CALVIN
Switzerland
Calvinism • Reformed Church (John Knox)
Presbyterians • French Huguenots • Congregational

Anglicanism (1534)

KING HENRY VIII
Great Britain
Church of England (Anglican Church)
Episcopal Church (U.S.A.)
Methodists (Wesleyans)
Salvation Army

Evangelicalism (1520)

ANABAPTISTS
Germany, the Netherlands
Baptists (U.S.A.) • Mennonites
Amish • Hutterites

CHURCH AUTHORITY

Though I feel proud for the strides made in organization and prestige of the Church of the Middle ages, I cringe in horror as I read of the politics, atrocities, and immorality of the popes of the Avignon and the Schism era and the worldliness of the Renaissance popes who forget their pastoral mission. I thank God for our pope today and pray that this integrity continues with future popes.

GREAT SAINTS

While despondent at the papal scandals, I regain composure and pride as I consider the giants of holiness this era produces. Bernard, Francis, Dominic, Thomas Aquinas, Catherine of Siena, Hildegard, and other mystics model for me the ideal. Their example challenges me, and I find inspiration in reading their works and accounts of their lives.

PIETY AND DEVOTION

Since the Church hierarchy does not give good example, the lay people of the Middle Ages keep the faith alive. The simplicity and sincerity of those who reverence relics, pray the rosary, take part in the processions, and live pious lives inspire me.

Although I cannot entirely resonate with the spirituality of the Middle Ages, I realize the people of that time have a vastly different view of the world. What we understand as natural and explained, they consider supernatural and miraculous. The faith and practices good for that era may not be meaningful today. While ideas and methods may differ, there is value in devotions and private prayer.

The Renaissance

As I reflect on the Renaissance, I appreciate the art and cultural legacy of that era, especially the Pietà, the Sistine Chapel, and magnificent Saint Peter's Basilica. I find Dante's *Divine Comedy* helpful to me in reflecting on my eternal destiny.

The Need for Reform

The Renaissance emphasizes human nature and slights traditional spiritual discipline. Just as I need a reality check when I get into a personal rut, so also the Church needs the reformers and their concern for inner renewal. In my spiritual journey, I too need reform and renewal. May my reflections on the Reformation era encourage me in my spiritual strivings toward renewal.

PART IV

The Church Today

The Catholic Reformation (1545) to the Present

Imagine yourself a Catholic after the Reformation. Catholicism is no longer the only religion in Western Europe but is one among many. The Protestant denominations spread to an insecure and unstable Europe. You long to remain steadfast in your faith, but reformers continue to circulate their ideas.

The Catholic Church wrestles with its own inner conflicts and need for renewal. Now more than ever it needs to defend and affirm the faith. Necessary reform from within does not come easily. How does the Church cope with this explosion of dissidence and turmoil? It answers the dilemma in a radical way. Pope Paul III takes a stand and initiates the Catholic Reformation when he calls together the Council of Trent, a major chapter in our Catholic Church story.

Catholic
Response
to the
Reformation:
The Council
of Trent
(1545-1563)

The leaders of the Catholic Church realize the need to deal with outside forces and the even more urgent need to initiate spiritual renewal from within. So Pope Paul III calls together the Council of Trent (1545-1563), from which the Church takes a defensive and disciplinary stance, correcting abuses and clarifying Church doctrines. With so much unrest caused by the reformers, Catholics need to know exactly where the Church stands on issues. This Council sets forth authentic Catholic teachings in a definitive way. It issues numerous directives concerning education of clergy, establishment of seminaries, and conduct of the liturgy. The council guarantees fidelity to the truth and corrects abuses. Robert Bellarmine and Peter Canisius compile a catechism, a synthesis of the teachings of the Church. Popes of high moral caliber effectively bring about stability by correcting abuses.

The Church strives to regain its stature through exterior reform. The Mass and rituals are regulated. Mass is in Latin and the congregation are observers, with little direct participation. The Bible is available in only Church-sanctioned translations, based on the Vulgate.

The laity supplement their spirituality through devotions and pious practices, many of which are carry-overs from the Middle Ages. Devotions to saints and veneration of relics become common among the laity.

Devotion to the Eucharist is enhanced by benedictions, Corpus Christi processions, and exposition of the Blessed Sacrament in ornate monstrances.

POPE SAINT PIUS V

Pope Saint Pius V (1566-1572), the only sixteenth-century pontiff canonized, brings a deep piety and integrity to the papal office. He implements the decrees of the Council of Trent, forbids nepotism, and challenges cardinals to moral integrity. An example of exemplary virtue, Pius V, a Dominican, continues to wear his religious habit. This tradition of the white Dominican cassock continues as the official papal garb.

GREGORY XIII

Gregory XIII (1572-1585), founds seminaries and encourages missionary activity. He is most remembered for his reform of the Julian calendar. In consultation with astronomers, Gregory develops a more accurate measurement of time. The Gregorian calendar rectifies the ten-day discrepancy between the lunar and solar cycles. October 5, 1582, becomes October 15, 1582. So trivia buffs, note that nothing happens in the world between October 5 and 15, 1582. The adjusted Gregorian calendar is now the universal gauge of time.

The post-reformation popes of the sixteenth century accomplish their aims of bringing the Church to a vitality and spirit of renewal. The laity too feel more confident and renewed in zeal.

Religious Orders Help Renew the Church

After the Reformation, new fervor inspires the formation of new religious orders. The Capuchins, a branch of the Franciscans, return to the original austere spirit of Francis and spread the faith as missionaries, confessors, preachers, and teachers.

Ignatius of Loyola (1491-1556) proves to be the dynamic driving force of reform. Wounded in battle, he undergoes a spiritual transformation and writes a guide for the spiritual life, *The Spiritual Exercises,* still popular today. His zeal attracts others to follow, and he founds the Society of Jesus, known as the Jesuits, who pledge fidelity to the pope. The Jesuits increase rapidly, specializing in education, mission work, and evangelization. They halt the advance of Protestantism and help to regain areas lost to Catholicism. Many of the theologians and missionaries of the post-Reformation are Jesuits.

Outstanding Jesuits include Francis Xavier, missionary to India, Japan, and the East. Matthew Ricci brings the faith to China by including Chinese customs with Catholicism. Later many Jesuits, for example, Pierre Marquette and Isaac Jogues, spread the faith in North America. Today the Jesuits labor in many parts of the world as one of the largest and best-known religious orders in the Church.

Vincent dePaul (1580-1660) founds the Congregation of the Mission, or the Vincentians as they are commonly known, who concentrate on charitable work for the poor and the sick. A lay movement, the Vincent de Paul Society, founded by Frederick Ozanam, still today contributes to the Church's outreach to the poor and needy.

Louise de Marillac founds the Sisters of Charity, an active, uncloistered woman's religious community, to work with the poor.

Since 1535 the Ursulines of Angela Merici are specialists in education.

Alphonsus Liguori (1696-1787), moral theologian known for his classic *The Glories of Mary,* establishes the Redemptorists, the Congregation of the Most Holy Redeemer, to work among the poor and provide spiritual guidance through missions and retreats around the world.

This post-Reformation period sees a popular style of religious life emerge as active religious communities labor in new areas and fields of ministry. Since the Church becomes more involved in the needs of the people, the active religious apostolate focuses mainly on charitable works, healthcare, and education.

Contemplative life thrives and produces giants of spirituality in Spain. Teresa of Avila and John of the Cross live at a time when the Inquisition tribunal still operates in Spain.

Teresa of Avila (1515-1582), a noted mystic, Doctor of the Church, spiritual writer, and Carmelite reformer, falls prey to the inquisitors, who respond to complaints of her reform efforts. We chiefly remember Teresa's spiritual legacy, *The Interior Castle,* a classic on prayer, and *The Way of Perfection.*

John of the Cross (1500-1569), also under scrutiny by the Inquisition, preaches a rigorous spirituality and serves as spiritual adviser to Teresa of Avila. His legacy includes mystical and spiritual writings, especially the perennial classic *The Dark Night of the Soul.*

Mystics of the Post-Reformation

While much of Europe experiences unrest and instability, a new enthusiasm springs forth as new frontiers open. Discoveries in other parts of the world, particularly the Americas, expand the Spanish, Portuguese, English, and French claims. A passage from Europe around Africa and South America opens the way to vast areas unexplored. Spain and Portugal lead the way in South America, Mexico, and the U.S. Southwest. France sends missionaries with explorers to Canada and the Mississippi River. Puritans and settlers from England claim New England and Virginia for the Protestants.

The Church overcomes inner turmoil and expands to mission lands. Jesuit, Franciscan, and Dominican missionaries accompany expeditions. Missionaries leave their mark in the American Southwest as they name Los Angeles, Santa Barbara, San Diego, Sacramento, San Juan, Santa Fe, and many others—a testimony to Catholic influence.

The New World

The Post-Reformation Church

The map of Europe after the Reformation is redrawn and reassembled according to religious persuasion. No longer are individual countries automatically one religion.

This situation brings about the wars of religion in France (1562-1568), political and religious disputes between Catholics and French Protestants, the Huguenots. The Edict of Nantes in 1598 settles the issue, granting freedom to the Huguenots.

But peace is not to endure. The Thirty Years' War (1618-1648) involves most European nations in religious dynastic and territorial squabbles. The Peace of Westphalia (1648) ushers in an era of peace but it also sows the seed of division with its provision that the ruler of the kingdom determines the religion of the land.

Wars fought in the name of religion take their toll on attitudes toward God. Several movements sweep across Europe, and of course the Church is inextricably intertwined.

Jansenism (1585-1638)

Cornelius Jansen, bishop of Ypres, Belgium, erroneously interprets Augustine's teaching about grace, preaches the inherent depravity of humans, and denies free will, creating a Catholic form of Calvinism. This leads to the heresy called Jansenism, which advocates moral austerity and a person's unworthiness to receive Communion due to sinful human nature. The Church denounces Jansen's extreme morality, yet the attitude persists in the minds of the laity. This thinking pervades France. In Germany it appears as Febronianism, in Austria as Josephism.

Although Pope Clement XI in 1713 condemns Jansenism, Catholics remain split on the issue. Its influence continues to this day, in those who uphold a rigorous and austere morality.

The reaction to Jansenism swings the pendulum the opposite way. It leads to ideas of the Enlightenment, in which human reason is supreme and faith is discounted.

Think now how the Reformation affected people's lives and attitudes. The instability of the Reformation with its proliferation of religious ideologies nurtures strong feelings of discontent and suspicion of spiritual things. As people are exposed to the claims of each reformer, they question and search for answers. The Church loses its monopoly on religion, and the reformers do much harm to its image. People seek anywhere for probable solutions to life's big questions.

This critical reevaluation of the role of religion ushers in the Age of Enlightenment in the 1700s. Faith and things religious are distrusted and looked at as outmoded and irrelevant to the times. Human reasoning becomes the ultimate norm for dealing with intellectual, political, scientific, and philosophical issues. The Enlightenment promises hope for scientific progress and encourages experimentation toward new knowledge. To understand the world, humans need to apply creative thinking and reasoning. This attitude breeds tolerance for new ideas and is a strong reaction against religious intolerance.

Scientific developments and explanations support the Enlightenment and discredit any supernatural explanations. Once religion is pushed aside, we see a spate of philosophers, scientists, and scholars who are proponents of the new thought and consider human knowledge to be based on reasoning and human creativity.

The Enlightenment: Reason Rather Than Faith

Galileo
(1564-
1642)

Take the example of Galileo. For centuries people believe that the earth is the center of the universe, taking the account of Genesis literally. But then a Polish astronomer, Nicholas Copernicus, says that the sun is the center of our galaxy. Galileo, a scientist and discoverer of the pendulum, the telescope, and the moons of the planets Jupiter and Venus, most ardently supports the Copernican theory of the sun as the center of the universe. Galileo publicizes his certainties, but the Church silences and imprisons him in 1633, because the Church considers the Copernican theory at that time heretical, contrary to biblical accounts of the creation in chapter one of Genisis. Time proves Galileo correct. In 1992 Pope John Paul II exonerates Galileo and expresses regret at his fate.

Rene
Descartes
(1596-
1650)

Descartes realizes science is beginning to transform civilization and society. He questions the reliability of the senses, doubts everything, and affirms personal existence in his famous statement, "I think, therefore I am." This theory leads to a rationalist approach to reality and brings religious issues into question.

Voltaire
(1694-
1778)

Voltaire sees deceit and corruption in the Church and with wry wit attacks it. He supports deism, a theory that acknowledges God as a creator but one who has no concern for the world, remaining indifferent to it. Only through use of reason and experience can human beings attain a perfect society. These deist views spread throughout Europe and into the American colonies, greatly influencing Thomas Jefferson and Benjamin Franklin.

Rousseau, philosopher and influential political theorist, proposes a secular theory of government. He contends that humans are good by nature but made corrupt by society and civilization. Rousseau's idea of laws and government based on the will of the people governed paves the way for the American and French Revolutions.

Philosophers and scientists explain away the spiritual and natural mysteries of life in rational ways. Human reason is seen as the supreme norm. Such is the atmosphere of the Church of the eighteenth century. The philosophers Locke and Berkeley teach that the senses are the norm for all religious expression. Descartes, Spinoza, Kant, and other rationalists preach the authority of natural reasoning and doubt the senses.

Imagine how these revolutionary ideas confuse ordinary people and affect their attitude toward life and government. The nobles are now not the only learned ones, but the laity become literate and feel more confident to express their feelings. Ordinary citizens, convinced of their rights, speak out. This attitude sets the stage for what is to become one of the most harrowing events of eighteenth-century Europe, the French Revolution.

On July 14, 1789, the people rebel and storm the Bastille, a prison and the symbol of French supremacy. The Reign of Terror ensues, the Church is attacked, churches and monasteries are closed, religious communities are dissolved, and many clergy and Catholics who are on the side of the revolution are guillotined.

Napoleon becomes dictator in 1799, and until 1815 there is unrest. To his personal advantage, he forges a concordat with the pope.

At the Battle of Waterloo in 1815, Napoleon is defeated, the Bourbon family resumes control, and there is a period of relative peace.

The French Revolution makes possible the democratic governments we experience today. The divine right of the monarchy is destroyed, and a new code of laws respects the individual and allows persons to rise above their class. The French Revolution's impact on the Church has long-reaching effects. It also influences our American founding fathers in 1789 when they guarantee freedom of religion in the First Amendment to the American Constitution.

Industrial-ization

The nineteenth century ushers in a world rapidly changing due to numerous inventions and ways of producing goods. The Industrial Revolution changes lifestyles and working conditions and profoundly affects the ordinary person. Skilled artisans' creativity is replaced by machinery and mass production. No longer working from the comfort of home in cottage industries, laborers are forced into crowded factories where child labor is common.

This Revolution not only affects society and our lifestyles but it also has theological implications. Technology affects our spiritual values and religious faith. The Church confronts new challenges in the fields of morality and social justice.

The Church in the 1800s

Although the Church is weakened during the Revolution and Napoleonic eras, a religious revival follows, with reverence for religious traditions and faith among the laity. Devotions and popular religion satisfy the hunger for a return to the spiritual. Missionary expansion continues with immigrants from Europe pouring into North America. The Church in North America grows.

Charles Darwin in 1859 opens another controversy with his *On the Origin of Species.* Darwin is a staunch proponent of the theory of evolution, that all forms of life evolve from lower forms. This theory, in contradiction to the account of creation in the first chapter of Genesis, raises questions about the origins of the human race and creates ongoing controversy between those who take the Bible literally and those who consider the Bible in its spiritual sense.

Pope Pius IX, the longest reigning and most significant pontiff of the nineteenth century, comes to office in 1846 during unrest and war. His thirty-two-year reign is highlighted in 1854 by the proclamation of the dogma of Mary's Immaculate Conception. Pius IX defines papal stability through Vatican Council I and the dogma of papal infallibility. Vatican I, cut short by the 1870 Franco-Prussian War, cannot conclude its discussion of bishops' roles. (This unfinished agenda is resumed by Pope John XXIII with Vatican II in 1962.) The Papal States become part of Italy. To protest the Italian government's settlement of the Papal States, Pius IX becomes a voluntary prisoner of the Vatican. This situation lasts until the Lateran Treaty in 1929.

Blessed Pope Pius IX (1846-1878)

The success of the Catholic Church in the latter part of the nineteenth century and in the twentieth century is due mainly to the leadership of the popes, who consider their spiritual and pastoral role a priority. The popes from Pius IX to the present show concern for the temporal and spiritual welfare of the people. Their personal lives and their awareness and concern in world affairs prove saintliness and leadership. Their varied backgrounds and distinct personalities embody the Church's universal nature. They lead the Church through turmoil in two world wars and through drastic change in lifestyles, political structures, technology, and communication.

You witness a new vitality in the nineteenth-century Church in many eminent saints, whose lives express a deep faith despite the turmoil of the times.

ELIZABETH SETON

Elizabeth Bayley Seton (1774-1821), the first Americanborn saint, is convert, wife, and mother. She founds the Sisters of Charity of Emmitsburg, Maryland. Her schools serve as models for Catholic parochial education in the United States.

JOHN NEUMANN

Bishop John Neumann (1811-1860), Redemptorist and bishop of Philadelphia, labors tirelessly in the eastern U.S., establishing numerous parishes.

JOHN VIANNEY

John Vianney, the Cure of Ars (1786-1859), parish priest and popular confessor, serves as an inspiration and consolation to French Catholics at a time of turmoil.

THÉRÈSE OF LISIEUX

Thérèse of Lisieux (1873-1897), "The Little Flower," is a Carmelite whose prayers for the missions earn her the title "Patroness of Missions."

FRANCIS CABRINI

Frances Xavier Cabrini (1850-1917), foundress of the Missionary Sisters of the Sacred Heart, works among Italian immigrants in the U.S.

The Church of the Council of Trent remains unchanged for four hundred years. This is the Church older Catholics fondly recall. It is defensive in preserving Catholic tradition, in which moral obligations are plainly spelled out. The "Is it a sin?" morality involves obeying rules and commandments. The Mass is the same everywhere, the rituals uniform. Authority rests with the pope as supreme head. Catholics accept the truths of faith unconditionally, no questions asked, for fear of excommunication. A Jesus-and-me piety predominates, through which people hope to save their souls and attain eternal salvation. The Church is the perfect society with all the answers. Membership in the Church is gauged by legal standards, external affiliation, and obedience to Church laws. Although this Church of Trent answers post-Reformation needs, the Church again needs reform in a world vastly different from that of the Trent era.

The Faith Before Vatican II

Pope Leo XIII ushers in the twentieth century with a different personality, temperament, and ideology than his predecessor. Leo XIII immerses himself in the cares and concerns of the people. Industrialization and mechanization affect drastically the way of living. This presents new challenges to the Church. Working conditions, poverty, labor unions, and just wages become concerns of the Church in the modern era. At this time when the Industrial Revolution changes lifestyles and working conditions, Leo XIII speaks out for the working class in his classic encyclical *Rerum Novarum* in 1891. He remains a prisoner of the Vatican after Italy confiscates the Papal States, and he keeps in touch with the world through his eighty-six encyclicals and thousands of letters.

Pope Leo XIII (1878-1903)

Pope Saint Pius X (1903-1914)

Saint Pius X, the first canonized pope since Pius V, brings a pastoral agenda to the papacy. Concerned for spiritual welfare and "restoring all things in Christ," Pius X advocates frequent Communion and makes it possible for children to receive Communion. He condemns Modernism, an attempt to explain Church teaching according to philosophical and scientific concepts. He is concerned with religious education for all and initiates the Confraternity of Christian Doctrine (CCD) for children in public schools. He inaugurates the revision of canon law, which is completed in 1917. To him we are grateful for his interest in Catholic action.

During his term the Church experiences a shift of populace through immigration. The Catholic population in the United States increases dramatically as the Irish flee the potato famine and others seek religious freedom. By 1908 the United States is no longer considered a mission country but a nation able to send missionaries to foreign lands. In 1911 the Missionary Society of America (known as Maryknoll) is founded and to this day is known for outstanding mission education and outreach.

Pope Benedict XV (1914-1922)

We remember Benedict XV in connection with World War I as absolutely impartial. His neutral stance is preoccupied with mediation and pleas for peace. Benedict provides positive relief for war victims and POWs and encourages the education of native clergy. The Code of Canon Law is promulgated in 1917. Benedict improves relations with France by canonizing Joan of Arc.

Pope Pius XI (1922-1939)

Pius XI comes to the papacy during negotiations to settle the "Roman Question," the status of Rome after Italy takes control of the Papal States. With the signing of the Lateran Treaty in 1929, Vatican City becomes an independent nation within the city of Rome, with its own coins and stamps. (This treaty is renegotiated in the 1980s. Requirements for compulsory Catholic education in Italian schools and for payment of clerical salaries by the Italian government are dropped.)

Raised in Rome as the son of a diplomat, Pius XII brings a dignity and elegance to the papacy. Although criticized for his silence concerning the Holocaust during World War II, Pius XII clandestinely harbors and saves the lives of numerous Jews from the Hitler regime.

Pope Pius XII (1939- 1958)

Pius XII's active pontificate is proven by his forty-one encyclicals and more than one thousand addresses. We cannot overlook Pius XII's significant contribution to modern biblical scholarship with the encyclical *Humani Generis,* which definitively states that Genesis is not a scientific theory but a statement of faith.

The declaration of the Assumption of the Blessed Virgin Mary as dogma in 1950 completes Marian theology. Pius XII anticipates Vatican II as he initiates liturgical changes concerning Eucharistic fast, dialogue Masses in which the laity respond, and Holy Week liturgy changes.

Recall images of the jolly friendly pontiff whom all thought too old and unable to do anything noteworthy. How wrong an assumption! Realizing that the First Vatican Council had never officially adjourned and that the Church needs updating to be an effective witness in the world, Pope John XXIII convenes the Second Vatican Council in 1962. Recently beatified, he is also remembered for his Christian unity efforts and his encyclical, *Peace on Earth,* the first addressed to all peoples, not only Catholics.

Blessed Pope John XXIII (1958- 1963)

Vatican II
and Its
Significance
for the
Church and
the World

The Second Vatican Council, the most significant religious event of the twentieth century, impacts all areas of Church life. With drastic innovations, it does not condemn or reject past Catholic practices and doctrinal expressions. The Council Fathers realize the Church is no longer effective in its mission, and they update outmoded practices. Vatican II issues no dogmatic or doctrinal proclamation; its primary thrust is pastoral and ecumenical. It defines the nature of the Church as the pilgrim people of God. The pope leads not alone but along with the bishops in collegiality. Ecclesial responsibility formerly reserved for the pope is shared by the bishops. Synods of bishops, regular convocations in Rome, and national conferences of bishops are genuine expressions of collegiality.

Vatican II focuses on the Church in the modern age. What needs change and what needs to be preserved as the Church's faith and tradition become the main concerns. To attain this objective, the sixteen council documents deal with every phase of Church life. The most striking changes can be seen in the celebration of Mass in the vernacular, the role of the laity, and greater tolerance and understanding of other religions.

*Pope Paul VI
(1963-
1978)*

Pope Paul VI reconvenes and implements Vatican II. He enacts liturgical reforms and restores the permanent diaconate, which permits married men to assist in liturgical capacity—preaching, administering baptism, and pastoral work. Of Paul VI's seven encyclicals, *Humanae Vitae* causes the most controversy, because the encyclical adamantly forbids artificial birth control. Known as "the pilgrim Pope" and the first pope to travel by air, Paul VI visits the Holy Land, India, Portugal, Turkey, South America, the Pacific Isles, Australia, and the

Philippines, where he survives an assassination attempt in 1970. In the interests of world peace, he addresses the United Nations in 1965.

Though his reign is only thirty-three days, this gentle, smiling pontiff gives nineteen addresses. He breaks tradition in his choice of a double papal name, refuses the coronation tiara, and is installed with the pallium, a symbolic woolen stole. He leaves us a literary legacy penned during his pastoral days, *Illustrissimi.* In it, he converses with historic and fictional characters and discusses what we learn from them.

Pope John Paul I (1978)

This pope steers the Church through the last quarter of the twentieth century and ushers in the new millennium. Being the first Polish pope and living through the hardships of a communistic society, John Paul is a pope for the ages, outspoken against violence and war, discrimination and modern atheism.

Pope John Paul II (1978-)

To adapt to the changing circumstances in the world, Pope John Paul II updates the Code of Canon Law in 1983 and in 1992 publishes a modernized *Catechism of the Catholic Church.*

John Paul II is the pope of firsts and mosts. He sports a wristwatch, goes skiing, publishes a play, and is a gifted linguist. He is the first pope to enter a mosque on his trip to Damascus, Syria, and he publicly begs forgiveness for the harm and injustices of the Church over the centuries.

Pope John Paul II canonizes more saints than all former pontiffs combined. He is the most traveled, having been to over one hundred countries in over ninety-three trips abroad. He survives an assassination attempt in 1981.

Poor health and advanced age do not deter him from papal duties, as he meets with leaders of all nations and all religions. Pope John Paul II is known for his devotion to Mary and his firm and orthodox guidance of the Church. He leaves behind a legacy hard to match.

The Church in each age has its stalwart witnesses. The twentieth century is no exception. I list contemporary Catholics, outstanding in their faith who inspire me in my spiritual journey.

DOROTHY DAY (1897-1980)

Convert to the faith and founder of the Catholic Worker movement, she is a powerful advocate of social justice.

SAINT KATHERINE DREXEL (1858-1955)

A wealthy heiress, she founds the Sisters of the Blessed Sacrament to work with Native Americans and African-Americans.

SAINT MAXIMILIAN KOLBE (1894-1941)

This Polish Franciscan priest imprisoned at Auschwitz volunteers to take the place of a young father who is to be executed.

THOMAS MERTON (1915-1968)

A Trappist monk at Gethsemane Abbey, Kentucky, Merton is a prolific spiritual writer of over sixty books and is an advocate of ecumenism and social justice. He is accidentally electrocuted in Bangkok while at an ecumenical conference with Buddhist monks.

BISHOP OSCAR ROMERO (1917-1980)

This bishop of San Salvador earns the enmity of the government by speaking out against injustices. He is martyred while saying Mass.

FULTON J. SHEEN (1895-1979)

Bishop of Rochester, New York, Sheen is a dynamic, popular preacher and pioneer in radio-TV evangelism, who reaches millions through the communications media.

SAINT EDITH STEIN (1891-1942)

Jewish convert, writer, and philosopher, she enters the Carmelites and becomes a victim of the Nazi regime, gassed at Auschwitz.

MOTHER TERESA OF CALCUTTA (1910-1997)

Founder of the Missionaries of Charity, she is a recipient of the Nobel Peace Prize for her untiring labors and dedication to the service of the sick, poor, and dying in India.

SISTER THEA BOWMAN (1937-1990), JOSEPH CARDINAL BERNARDIN (1928-1996), AND JOHN CARDINAL O'CONNOR (1920-2000)

These Church leaders and writers show us not only how to live, but how to die. As cancer victims, their written experiences prove to be valuable legacies.

You may know others whose lives inspire you. Why not compile your own list?

Imagine yourself a Catholic returning to the Church after years of estrangement. Your remodeled parish church sports a wheelchair ramp. A side chapel serves for weekday Masses, perpetual adoration, and exposition of the Blessed Sacrament. You notice fewer statues and a simple altar table facing the people.

You hear a commentator greet the assembly, and you see lay ministers take part in the entrance procession. The celebrant faces the people, and a deacon and acolytes assist at the altar. The congregation sings hymns you know from Protestant radio programs. A lay lector reads the epistle, and a cantor invites all to respond to the psalm.

The homilist updates you on ways in which the Church proclaims the Good News to the world and stresses the Church as healer, sacrament, and sign of Christ, a community of faith, and a pilgrim Church, still imperfect and growing. The homily helps you see the Church of the twentieth century.

A family offers the gifts of bread and wine. You respond to the prayers and join hands in the Our Father. You offer a sign of peace to those around you and receive communion in your hand and the cup from eucharistic ministers. A meditation period allows time for silent reflection and prayer. You experience the Mass differently and feel a part of it. After Mass you are warmly greeted by the lay ministers and priest and share refreshments. How different from days gone by when you hardly knew anyone, and you couldn't wait to rush out of church. You resolve to read more about the changes so that Sunday Mass can become for you a meaningful beginning for the week ahead.

You browse through the bulletin of the Church's activities. So many innovations and new activities! The

Church of today is so different from the Church you left years ago.

The pastor is the only priest and is responsible for two parishes in outlying areas.

A deacon, a married business executive, does pastoral work in the parish.

You see changes in the way in which the community prepares for and celebrates the sacraments. Mandatory preparation classes are scheduled for baptism and matrimony. Confession, now the sacrament of reconciliation, takes place not in a dark confessional but in a reconciliation room, with options for confession face to face or behind a screen. The Eucharist is brought regularly to the sick and homebound by parish visitors. A communal anointing of the sick and healing Mass is offered for anyone ill or aged. It is no longer only the "last rites." The confirmation class is reminded of their service projects.

Lay people have responsible roles in the parish. Lay teachers staff the school; catechists conduct the religious education and RCIA for converts; a business administrator tends to the parish finances; lectors, altar servers, cantors, and eucharistic ministers serve the community at the liturgy and in many other ways.

Married people, parents, senior citizens, teens, young adults, singles, the widowed, elderly, and homebound—all have opportunities through the parish to minister and be ministered to.

It seems Catholics today have opportunities not only to attend Sunday Mass but also to be involved in spiritual growth and enrichment through Eucharistic adoration, Bible study, prayer groups, retreats, support groups, and adult education.

The Church reaches out and attends to the needs of all through a soup kitchen, day-care center, hospice care, and food bank located in the large, now vacant convent. Because of the dearth of vocations, Sisters in ministry live in a small apartment.

An inter-religious prayer service and dialogue in a Protestant church is a welcome change. You can still recall the days when Catholics never set foot inside a Protestant church.

The parish church also has a Website to list other activities. This is the Church where you belong. How blessed to be back! Alive! Active! Vibrant! Living! Doing the work of Jesus!

This is the Church of Vatican II, a Church renewed, but a Church on pilgrimage.

Reflecting on the Last Five Hundred Years

As I reflect on the Church from the post-Reformation till today, I marvel at the miracle of the Church's survival. The Catholic Church, like the legendary phoenix, overcomes obstacles and springs back to a more vibrant and vital faith. This proves the Holy Spirit guides the Church through each difficult situation. After every setback, the Church revives stronger and more determined.

Papal Leadership

Consider the forty-eight popes after the Reformation. Each century has given us popes of sterling character and outstanding in holiness, although only two popes since the reformation have been canonized, Pius V and Pius X, and three are beatified, Innocent XI, Pius IX, and John XXIII. Catholics can be proud that we can look for guidance to a leader respected the world over. We may at times not agree with papal decisions, yet we look to the popes for leadership and guidance. I thank God for the wisdom and integrity of our post-Reformation popes. I pray that the next elected pope will continue making the Church a viable witness.

HEROIC WITNESSES

I believe we Catholics are blessed with the witness of hundreds of sincere believers who lived their Catholic faith to a heroic degree. The vitality of the Church depends on the many religious orders who work tirelessly in areas all over the world. Of the hundreds of religious communities founded after the Reformation, many still carry on their noble work.

I pray for the thousands of Catholics who gave their lives as martyrs, not only the canonized ones of which there are scores, but the unsung heroes of the wars of religion, the French Revolution, and the concentration camps of World War II.

WORLDVIEW

I think of how the world changed within the last five hundred years of the Catholic Church story. Each age has its unique challenges. How different the world today than the one Jesus referred to: "Go therefore and make disciples of all nations" (Matthew 28:19a)—from the hills of Galilee to all corners of the earth and beyond into cyberspace and interplanetary space.

INVOLVEMENT IN THE WORLD

The Church today is a voice of concern for social justice, respect for life at all stages, political rights, and the disadvantaged. How can I as a Catholic promote these concerns of the Church?

Appreciation of Scripture

Catholics since Vatican II are rediscovering the Bible. Although the Bible was translated into many languages before Trent, the Church's caution about authentic versions caused the Bible to be put into the background. Now Catholics are encouraged to study and pray with the Bible as an integral part of Catholic Christian faith.

Moral Issues

The Church is far from being fully reformed. In this modern world, the Church faces many issues, unheard of in years gone by. Consider genetic engineering, cloning and other reproductive issues, stem-cell research, life support systems. Catholics today need be cognizant of responsible moral responses to amazing medical breakthroughs that carry significant moral implications. Other questions remain in the realm of speculation toward which the Church has no stance at present—for example, life on other planets.

Challenges

The moral and ethical dimensions of scientific advances present a whole array of challenges and the need to discover God's plan for us. How does our present life further the spiritual realm? How can the Church respond to these outside forces? Our Church family has many internal challenges. How can the Church welcome all cultures? How do parishioners support a variety of spiritualities that exist within one parish? How can the Church effectively be an instrument of growth and spiritual support to the variety of age groups and ethnic diversities? How can the Church be a harbinger of peace in areas torn asunder by religious strife and hatred? How can the

Church continue its mission if there are so few vocations to the priestly and religious life? How can the Church answer the spiritual and physical needs of our day and age? Although we are an advanced society, the challenges are at times greater than in previous ages. These are issues unresolved and still affecting the tenor of the Church. No matter how we mortals struggle over such problems, we can rest assured that the future of the Church is in good hands—the hands of God. Jesus has promised, "I am with you always" (Matthew 28:20b).

As we conclude our pilgrimage, we realize this pilgrimage is not merely at an end. It invites us to continue in our own call to follow and make visible the mission of Jesus in the world. We each have our niche, and the way we make the Church alive is to be witnesses to what Jesus has urged, "The Good News must…be proclaimed to all nations" (Mark 13:10). We each in our own way can make this come true in our lives. The Church is as strong as the People of God. Look into your life. How are you furthering the reign of God on earth? In what way is the Church having a better impact on the world through your presence and efforts?

Reflection at the End of Pilgrimage

The future of the Church is in our hands today. We are writing the history of the Church, living in a time when we cannot turn inward and passively await the end time.

The world needs a spiritual guide and a reminder of God's reign on earth. May we continue to do our share to build up the body of Christ in the world. Amen

Resources

Bokenkotter, Thomas. *A Concise History of the Catholic Church*. NY: Doubleday, 1977.

Bunsen, Matthew. *Encyclopedia of Church History*. Huntington, IN: Our Sunday Visitor, 1995.

Catholic University. *New Catholic Encyclopedia*. NY: McGraw Hill, 1967.

Collins, Michael, and Matthew Price. *The Story of Christianity*. NY: DK Publishers, 1999.

McBrien, Richard P., ed. *The HarperCollins Encyclopedia of Catholicism*. NY: Harper Collins, 1995.

Pennock, Michael. *The Catholic Church Story*. Notre Dame, IN: Ave Maria Press, 1991.

Stravinskas, Peter, ed. *OSV Catholic Encyclopedia*. Huntington, IN: Our Sunday Visitor, 1991.